ARCHITECTURAL
ALPHABET

Geometria   Architectura   Pictura   Sculptura

Christian Friederich Carl Alexander.   Friederica Carolina.

ARCHITECTO-
NISCHES
ALPHABETH
bestehend
In Dreÿssig Grund u. Auff=Rissen
dann
Zwanzig Kaysserlich Koenigliche
Chur und Hoher Fürsten-Nahmen
in Grund und Auff=Rissen
nebst
einer Erklaerung über jeden Riss
einer Vorrede und Dedication
Diese
noch niemahlen zum Vorschein
gekommene Bau-Risse
sind in vielen Iahren zusamen
gezeichnet und auf eigene Kosten
herausgegeben
von

Iohann David
Steingruber,
Vieljaehrig Hochfürstlich Onolz-
bachischen Bau Inspectore.

D.A. Hauer Sculp.

JOHANN DAVID STEINGRUBER

ARCHITECTURAL ALPHABET

1773

Thirty-three plates reproduced in facsimile
The text translated by E. M. Hatt

WITH AN INTRODUCTION
AND SOME ACCOUNT OF
STEINGRUBER'S LIFE & WORK

BY

BERTHOLD WOLPE R.D.I.

GEORGE BRAZILLER
NEW YORK

Published in the United States in 1975
by George Braziller, Inc.

First published in a Limited Edition
by The Merrion Press, London, in 1972
Translation and editorial matter
© copyright 1972 by The Merrion Press

Standard Book Number: 0–8076–0751–7
Library of Congress Catalog Number: 74–76329
Printed in the United States of America
First Printing

DEDICATED TO THE MEMORY

OF

DAVID FARRANT BLAND

1911–1970

CONTENTS

INTRODUCTION

JOHANN DAVID STEINGRUBER (1702–87) was a practising architect and master builder at his native Ansbach,[1] in Bavaria, and for many years he acted as chief architect at the office of works for the whole principality. He was closely involved in replanning the townscape of Ansbach and, on a smaller scale, he was concerned in the design and building of some two hundred and fifty houses and more than fifty churches in the region, many of which still survive. Steingruber wrote three[2] other books on architectural and building subjects, all practical and serious, with handsome copper engravings. *Architectural Alphabet* was his fourth and last book and is something of a triumph of imagination and ingenuity. It was in contemplation and preparation for many years, and he published it slowly and in parts. Each letter of the Roman alphabet forms the basis of a stately and spacious baroque building, and thirty designs are provided to cover the twenty-five letters, with I serving for I and J, and alternatives for letters A, M, Q, R, and X.

Steingruber began publication of the *Architectural Alphabet* at his own expense in his seventy-first year in 1773.[3] He issued a two-page prospectus, now even rarer than the book, in which on 21 April 1773 he stated that for some years he had worked on this project and now issued the first part, plates II, III, VI, VIII, and IX. If it was acceptable to subscribers they could have further instalments of five plates each at 10 Kreuzer Rhenish,[4] and also special designs based on the names of the Margrave Alexander and his consort Friederica Carolina,[5] each at 20 Kr. Rhen.; in addition a design of a larger size based on the name of the emperor at 30 Kr. Rhen. which, when folded, could be bound[6] into the book. The very last instalment would also have the title and foreword attached.[7]

He quotes from Abbé Laugier:[8] 'Nothing demonstrates the lack of genius, the sterility of inventive powers of our architects more clearly than the eternal sameness that prevails in the laying-down of ground plans.' Steingruber himself continues: 'Furthermore, I think it not inappropriate—as so many imposing churches and convents have been dedicated to patron saints—that such buildings should be laid out according to the initial letters of their names . . ., and I have also seen designs of existing gardens, where names of princes and others have been planted

Notes numbered in the text appear on pages 104–109.

on the ground. It should not be unseemly and impossible in laying out a building belonging to a great lord for the name of the patron to be brought into the ground plan.' (See also p. 92.)

When the book was completed, with its final instalment he issued the foreword on 12 March 1774 in the form of an address to the reader. This document of six pages is heavy with biblical and classical allusion, and most of it seems to have little bearing on the matter that is being introduced. However, towards the end of the piece, Steingruber justifies his enterprise in this way:

'To my knowledge, however numerous the inventions of architectural schemes and layouts, no one has as yet worked on the idea of basing contours and ground plans on the letters of the Latin alphabet. So I have devoted my leisure hours, and with no detriment to the many official commissions graciously entrusted to me, to an attempt to compile a volume of such alphabet-based designs.

'Now it may well be argued against me that great lords are not likely to erect their palaces and other buildings on such plans as these and that I have indulged in this effort in vain. I can only reply that:

'1. All innovations serve some purpose, and this is especially true in the realm of architecture, for the ingenuity that is called for inspires and encourages research along other lines.

'2. The plans may well be serviceable when sites are most irregular in shape, offering to the architect the opportunity to explore all kinds of ways and means.

'3. The very quirks and curves of the letters may compel the architect to divide up his interiors more imaginatively, each maintaining its appropriate proportions; this factor alone undoubtedly has its advantages, not only for the industrious beginner but also for the architect with years of practice behind him—especially is this so because I have supplemented each of the letter-based plans by a careful description in order to make the work more generally useful.'

Steingruber's *Architectural Alphabet* may seem startling in its conception but it is a characteristic product of the fantasy and exuberance of the baroque.[1] The extent of his achievement becomes more apparent when we think of the obstacles to architectural harmony imposed by the letter-forms: the uncompromising angularities, the sudden narrowing-down or closing-off of areas, the long arms making 'ribbon developments' inescapable, the connecting balconies and galleries representing transverse strokes, the oddly-shaped rooms at junctions and at crannies. Yet it will often be seen that the solutions proposed to these problems might indeed inspire other architects, even when they are working without such restraints. The tail of the Q, the loop of the P and D, the protuberant middle of the E, the intractable curves of the O—all such drawbacks he turned to advantage.

Introduction

When, as with I, the difficulties were extreme, he wisely permitted himself a proper degree of licence, and so honoured his commitment to his readers and his obligations to his distinguished patrons.

Many of Steingruber's devices were too useful to be abandoned after only one or two exploitations. There were the stairways, for instance: spiral, dog-leg, turret, *de dégagement*, perron, double, or purposely insignificant. Some effectively divert the eye from long rows of windows and masonry blocks; some give access to other floors without encroaching much on living space; others shorten inconvenient distances between kitchens and dining-rooms.

Heating plans, too, were ingenious. Family and retinue had to be kept warm: in the statelier rooms there were hearths and chimneys, but elsewhere stoves had to be placed close to both apartments and corridors, but unobtrusively, so that the business of stoking might be carried on discreetly from outside.[1]

Naturally enough, as a man of his time Steingruber was satisfied with somewhat meagre locations for necessary offices and domestic staff's quarters, being more generous in his provision for horses and their accoutrements. There is always sensible allowance made for bakehouses and wine cellars.

We find evidence here and there that this expert practitioner, designing and writing in a fairly relaxed mood, is not ashamed of having second thoughts. But there are several occasions when it would be enlightening to know for certain which storey of the building was under discussion, and where exactly the architect proposed to add a symbol or lower-case letter which finally was overlooked by the engraver. One can follow his mind at work when he innocently gives his second version of A with a naïve admission that the first A, as was usual, was too acutely pointed, a matter set right in the second design. Elsewhere second versions are offered for quite other reasons: the popularity of the initial M among great personages makes it advisable to have a choice of plan; the asymmetry of the first design of R is ingeniously countered in the second; in the case of Q he is tempted to depart from his principle of respecting the letter-form at all costs, and attempts to balance the tail by adding a blind entrance, which is for Steingruber far from being a typical solution. Most projects in the book are planned to be built on level ground, but in contrast the one based on the letter Q makes good use of a sloping hillside. Steingruber seems particularly pleased with his splendid mountain castle with its abundance of terraced gardens and orangeries. As approached from lower ground level its masonry looks fairly tall and impressive (Plate XVIII). Turning to the next plate it comes as a surprise to find the building drawn in section to give a view of all four floors. A courtyard surrounded by open arcades on two floors and a mansard roof all around promises plenty of light and air, and provides a light-hearted effect which the palace's severe exterior does not lead one to expect. Wherever Steingruber gives a second version of a letter, it is for a good practical reason, and it is obvious throughout that the best possible exploitation of all usable space has been an overriding consideration. That clarity of outline was important to him is stressed in his description of the building based on the letter T, easily recognizable when viewed from its narrow end; here he insisted again that in most other cases the ground plan became clear when the building was seen from the top of a hill or a tower.

It was his usual practice to show the façade as though viewed from the foot of the letter, but in the case of E he realized that a departure was necessary. Why did he not introduce a little more variety then, for the letter L? His façades seem to have concerned him less than the disposition of interior space, and at first sight they appear somewhat unadventurous and often virtually interchangeable. That is, unless the letter shape induced him to choose a bolder treatment of roofs. The wholesale acceptance here of conventional proportions, the readiness to adorn with central and corner domes, or with electoral, symbolic, and other types of ornament, the almost casual mixing of orders, doubtless constituted Steingruber's bow to accepted custom. Just as certainly, once behind the façade, he bowed only to his own delighted but always practical invention.

Undoubtedly he enjoyed his skill in making the best use of the restricted space provided within the letter-forms. By abandoning the contrast between thick and thin of traditional capitals he made a bold, even-stroke alphabet the basis of all these designs. Fully-fledged serifs would have been entirely out of place, but by slightly curving out the corners he succeeded in giving the edges of his buildings that emphasis so rightly valued by the experienced craftsman, whatever his medium. Steingruber also offers us, on the intricate engraved title page, a bold sans-serif alphabet[1] ahead of its time, and it is fascinating to find that this engraved title piece shows also, in its two-column alphabet crowned by his patrons' initials, a well-organized synopsis of the whole book.[2]

From minor touches here and there, it is clear that gardens of the Le Nôtre type and the 'proper Knottes' esteemed in Tudor times and described, for instance, by Thomas Hill,[3] might easily have been allied with some of Steingruber's letter-based buildings if the distinguished occupants were so inclined. In a similar spirit 'knots' and light-hearted pen flourishes were much used to embellish ordinary handwriting and lettering. Whether or not he was aware of it, Steingruber was not a complete innovator.[4] The Roman capital, in the shape of his own initials, served John Thorpe (*c.* 1565–*c.* 1651) as ground plan for a group of buildings which he designed as his own residence. We do not know whether the plans were ever translated into stone or brick, but Horace Walpole, who owned the book of Thorpe's drawings, while disparaging his use of ornament concedes that 'there is judgment in his disposition of apartment and office, and he allots most ample space for halls, staircases, and chambers of state'.[1]

In his book of essays on architecture which was projected but never actually built,[2] Josef Ponten wrote pleasantly and sympathetically of the designs in Steingruber's *Architektonisches Alphabet*, describing them as being far more 'buildable', practicable and feasible than, for instance, the hare-brained schemes of the Frenchman Gobert,[3] whose architectural designs were based on the letters of LOUIS LE GRAND and then doubled mirrorwise. We may assume, from Steingruber's own assessment of the originality of his undertaking, that he had not come across Gobert's work. Ponten admired many aspects of Steingruber's plans, mentioning in particular the S-shaped castle, the undaunted exploitation of the most awkward features of the M and X, the covered carriageway into the courtyard which characterizes Q, and above all the faithful adherence to eighteenth-century practice. Ponten made no secret of his delight in certain diverting aspects of the castles based on the initials of princelings, and pretended to be baffled (although 'sauce for the goose is sauce for the gander') that there should be a castle for the princess as well. Maybe, he ventured, one was for winter, one for summer; one for days and one for nights; but, he concludes, what does it matter, for on paper they cost nothing.

Nothing is reported of how the *Architectural Alphabet* was received when it was dedicated and probably given to the Margrave Alexander, but it is interesting to find that at the festivities in honour of the nuptials in 1754 of Margrave Alexander and Princess Friederica Carolina of Coburg the food was served from a table representing the interlaced letters F C. We know that Steingruber gave a copy of his book to the town hall in Ansbach, where it was passed on to the *Registratur* for safe keeping. It was decreed that he should be given a *douceur* of twelve Gulden[4] from the town chest, and the book has been preserved to this day in the town library and archives.[5]

Although the title page of *Architectural Alphabet* gives 1773 as the date of publication, the address to the reader is dated: Anspach, twelfth of March 1774. According to the typographic title page the work was to be published in three instalments—a change from the prospectus of 1773 (see p. 11). The editor's copy, which belonged to a member of the Steingruber family,[6] has a typographic section title for the second series of fifteen letter-forms in the middle of the book (see p. 102), an indication that the thirty plates and their descriptive text were brought out at two separate dates.[7] This leaf is missing from most surviving copies. It is of some importance, as it tells us of Steingruber's future publishing plans, announcing a third instalment of eighteen[8] further plates based on the names (initials, we

ARCHITECTURAL ALPHABET

Consisting of Thirty Designs

Each letter of the alphabet is, in accordance with its distinguishing
features, disposed in the form of a stately and spacious princely
residence; or, serving various creeds, in the form of palace chapels,
and in one case a monastery, but for the most part according to German usage
with stoves for heating and only occasionally chimney-pieces,
and additionally,
in consequence of the more irregular 'ground plans' (which certain
letters innately possess), several kinds of main staircase and service
stairs the like of which are not commonly found in architectural plans,
and to these features are added the façades, which are planned with a
marked variety of architectural elements.
Furthermore,
there are twenty plans* in the names of imperial, royal, electoral
and other personages of high nobility, based on similar ground plans
and with utmost assiduity and in distinguished architectural language
set out each on one sheet, so that they may be bound together
with the aforementioned plans in a single format.
In their case, as in the case of the first set of designs,
a detailed explanation, with a special introduction and title-page
and dedication, are appended.
These designs, delineated over many years, and never before published,
are presented, at his own expense, in three instalments,
to those learned in architecture and to curious readers
for their discriminating judgment and kind acceptance
by
JOHANN DAVID STEINGRUBER
for many years Inspector of Buildings
to the Prince of Brandenburg-Anspach

SCHWABACH
Printed by
JOHANN GOTTLIEB MIZLER,
Printer by appointment to the Prince

1773

* Only two of these plans were issued. See note 11.5

Explanation of the Plan and Elevation
based on the Initials of the Name of
His Serene and Illustrious Highness
the reigning Margrave of Brandenburg-Onolzbach
and Bayreuth, etc.

CHRISTIAN FRIEDERICH CARL ALEXANDER

ALTHOUGH at first sight, and from the introductory words to the first designs based on the letters of the alphabet, this undertaking might well be esteemed an unnecessary and idle one—thus to place before the eyes of people of discernment this unliteral use of letters, these architectural schemes deriving from a whole name, this eccentric building procedure—yet it cannot be denied that bees sip the delicious and profitable honey from many and varied flowers; so that from ground plans that also are many and varied, with their manifold and widely contrasting details, might not some idea or another perchance be culled and put to good use, especially by a novice? And it is not beyond the bounds of possibility that a splendid edifice would result. To quote the Abbot Laugier, in his *Notes on Architecture*, 'There is not sufficient variety in the forms of buildings, but just endless monotony.' In this respect, the present project for a tripartite building can be described in this way.

The middle block is based on three letters, on a rectangular site, with two Fs and an A in the centre representing the *corps de logis*; and the two Cs are the two outer ranges of buildings. The following details of layout should be observed: the mark ☉ [sun sign] in the middle of A is the outer court, with (*a*) grand entrance, to right and left of which are (*b*) two vestibules of irregular shape, and beyond (*c*) the hall at the foot of the (*d*) staircases, and adjoining (*e*) the main corridors to (*f, g, h, i, k*) the apartments farther on beyond the stairs, leading to (*l, m, n*) other chambers; and between these sets of rooms, (*o*) the ordinary dining-room. At the far end of the aforementioned corridors (*e*) the letter-form is closed off in (*p*) another vestibule, oval in shape. Below this and its entry is the mark ☽, a small courtyard of irregular shape; then, from the vestibule (*p*) the entrance to (*q*) the oval-shaped great hall with (*r, s, t, u*) chambers to both right and left, for guests and for use as visiting rooms, each wing ending in (*v*) a small music-room. Note, too, that to right and left at the bottom, next to the outer court, are (*w*) two matching doors to areas and rooms at (*x*) serving as *garderobes*. Behind these, in the passages (*e*), concealed stairs and *Comoditaet* [closet].

This kind of imposing edifice should have cellars, kitchen, and other essentials arranged in the *souterrain*.

In front of the two side buildings C, at marks ♂ and ☿, large courtyards, of irregular shape, and in each half, at (*aa*) stables, with stalls for 41 horses, and in the centre (*bb*) a pavilion at the curve, used for grooming and shoeing of horses, and in the two corners (*cc*) wide spiral stairs. In the other two corners (*dd*) closets, then (*ee*) through a passage, (*ff*) two heatable rooms, and thereafter (*gg*) the oval-shaped riding-school, and beyond, (*hh*) two latrines; and at Mark ♃ [not shown in engraving] the way out. In the storey over the stabling and riding-school there would be lofts for storing fodder, and lodging for the grooms, also the saddle-room. In the second side building, mark ☿ (as aforementioned) is (ii) a pavilion, also placed centrally, and of service both for (*kk*) stalls for the horses, and (*ll*) if need be, for the orangery. In an upper floor there could likewise be store-rooms for fodder, and over the orangery a store-room for seeds and perhaps a gardener's lodging too.

Single and double pilaster strips run right through the two lower storeys of the *corps de logis* and flank the windows without elaboration. The attic storey is similar. At the two salient corners in the forecourt are twin turrets with a plain cupola surmounted by an urn. Principal and secondary buildings have a German [pitched] roof, but over the great hall is a stepped dome with an elector's crown. The central entry (*a*) and its two forecourts (*b*), representing the crossbar of the A, only one storey high, form a balustraded terrace uniting the wings; the balustrade pedestals are adorned with trophies and figures.

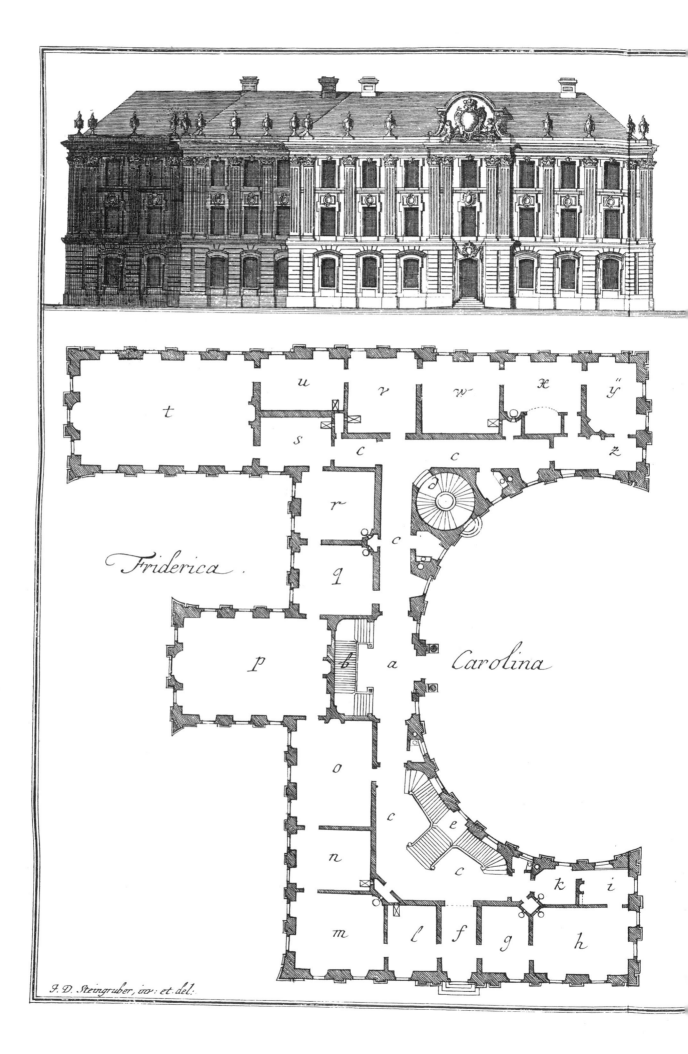

Friderica.

Carolina

G. D. Steingruber, inv: et del:

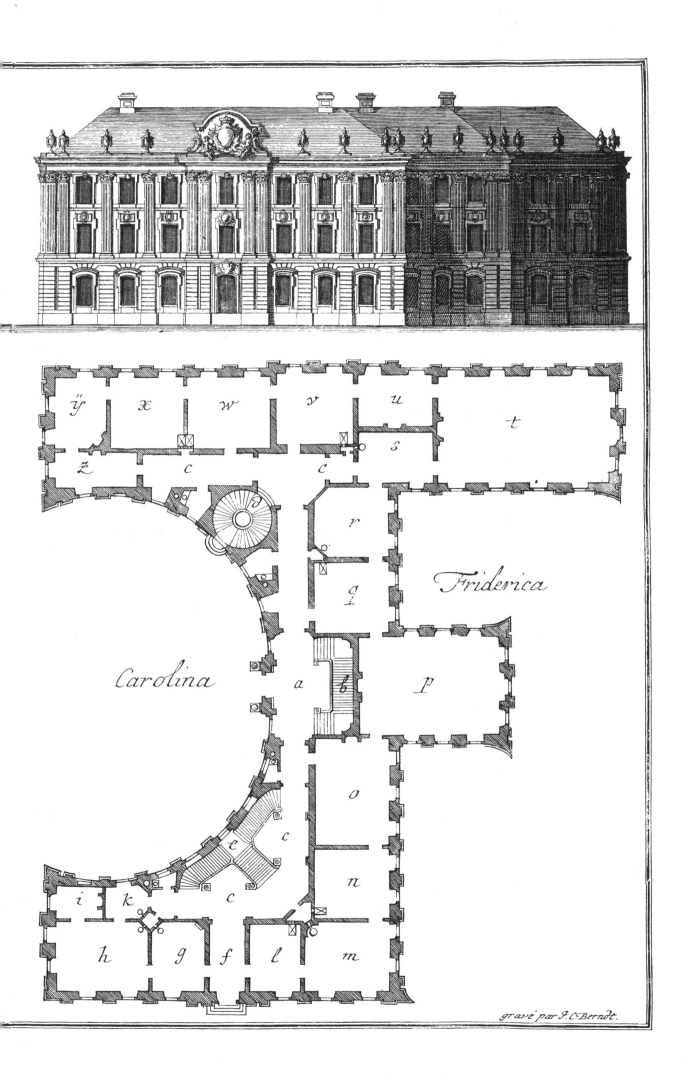

Friderica

Carolina

gravé par J. C. Berndt.

I . A

CONSIDERING this letter, we freely admit that from the very outset we have followed the shape too slavishly and topped our buildings with too sharp an angle, and, because of the two long arms resulting therefrom, interior angles proved to be excessively acute, so that (*a*) the great hall had to be set back further within the building, and accordingly in the lower angles beyond the aforementioned hall must be (*b*) the entrance and therein direct lighting to give sufficient visibility; however, in the upper angle there would be (*c*) a small *cabinet*, and on each side of it (*d*) the buffets. Then, below the main hall, on both sides of it, (*e*) two oddly-shaped *cabinets* with cylindrical stoves, and adjoining each of these (*f*) a bedchamber with alcove, behind which (*g*) a heating arrangement which warms hall, *cabinets*, and bedchambers; (*h, i*) two living-rooms with stoves, fed from (*k*) the main corridor. At the point where the cross-stroke of the A joins the two wings is (*l*) a passage-way, and on each side, (*m*) a vaulted way, one storey high, surmounted by balustraded galleries. To right and left run (*n*) the main stairways. Behind these, (*o*) two small rooms, the first with an open fireplace whereas the other two are (*p*) adjoining (*q*) large rooms with stoves in each. Below is (*r*) another apartment [in each wing] and (*s*) a spacious *cabinet* and (*t*) a wardrobe [or dressing-room] which could be heated by a stove connected to heating arrangements elsewhere. In the corridor are (*u*) a small stairway and a secret chamber.

And since a building of this size must have its kitchen, cellar, and other essential offices, these are placed in the lower level and excluded from the first-floor plan.

The façade is massive, with *refends* [masonry raised and recessed], and there is a German [pitched] roof.

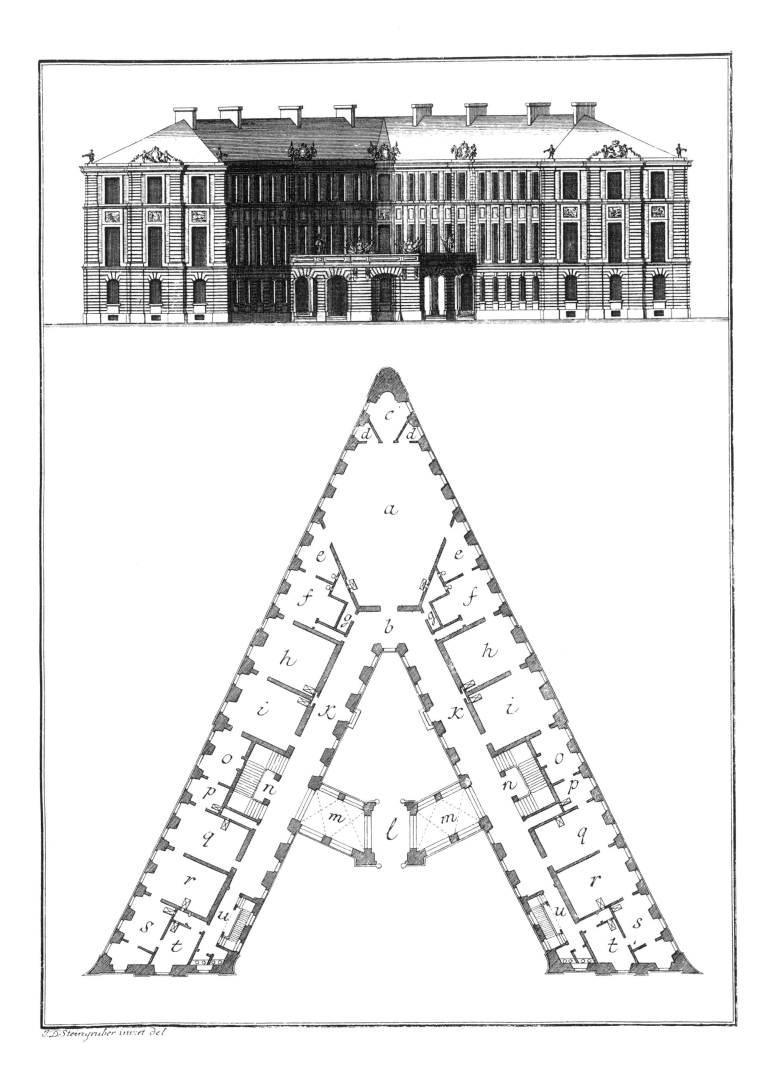

II . SECOND A

As the former A had already been engraved, it has been retained as a starting-point, but it has also been redesigned because of the aforementioned over-acute angle, in the hope that this new arrangement will find more ready acceptance.

The great hall (*a*) is right at the top, with an entrance, and semi-circular flight of steps, and also at the far end and in the broken corners on each side are niches for statues (*b*); and the connecting passage (*c*) leads away from the hall through both wings. Adjoining the aforementioned hall area are two irregularly-shaped rooms (*cabinets*) of fair size (*d*), and beyond these a *garderobe* (*e*) warmed, as are the hall and *cabinets*, by the heating arrangement (*d*). The two adjoining chambers (*f* [and *g*]) take heat from the same system by the agency of two iron stoves. Preserving the letter-form there is a central passageway (*g*) [this should be *h*] and on each side of it arcaded hallways (*h*) [this should be *i*] one storey high and linked at the top with railings made of iron or a stone balustrade. From the hallways just described run the two main flights (*i*) [this should be *k*] through the corridor immediately in view. Behind the rooms just mentioned are *cabinets* (*k*) [this should be *l*], with fireplaces, and beyond these again other large rooms (*l*) [this should be *m*], then bedchambers (*m*) [this should be *n*] with alcove, heated on both sides from the system (*n*) [this needs no letter] passing between. At the end of each wing is another *cabinet* (*o*) and roomy *garderobe* (*p*). In the corridor a secret stairway (*q*) and a closet (lavatory).

Above the passage [through the crossbar of the A] and the two vaulted hallways is the arcaded terrace connecting the wings. The façade is simple. Kitchens and cellars and other service rooms for such an establishment are much as described for the first A, completing a building of like magnitude, with a lower floor similarly contrived.

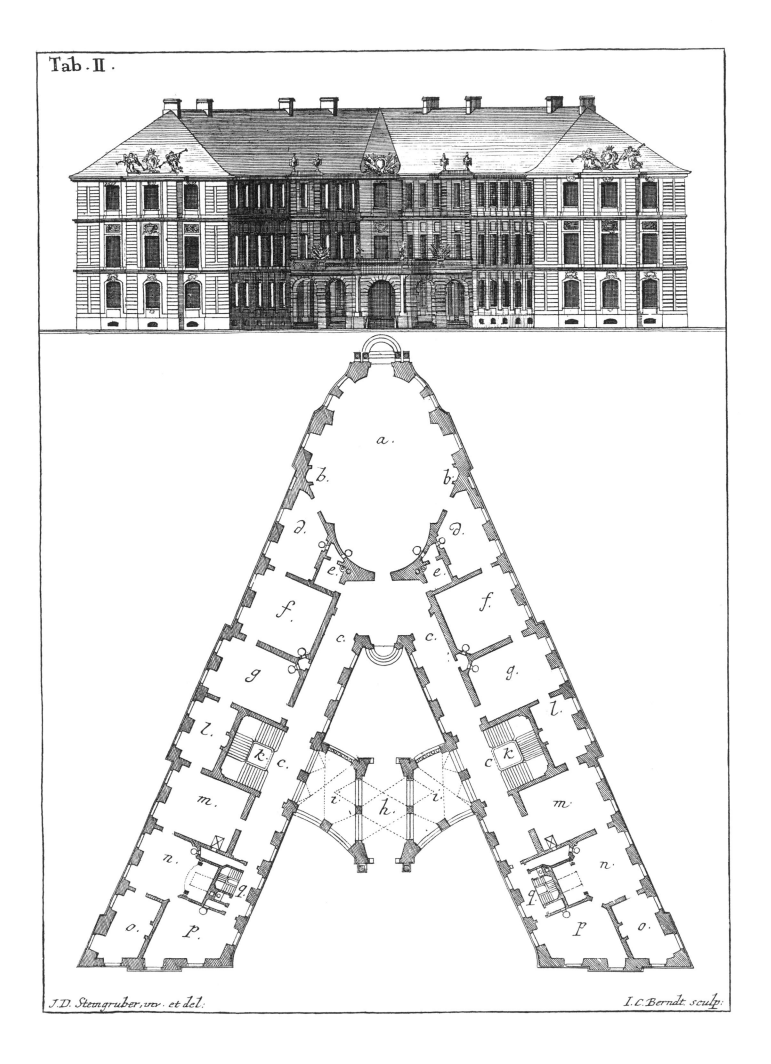

Tab. II.

J.D. Steingruber, inv. et del:

I.C. Berndt sculp:

III . B

WITHIN its two arcs this figure encloses two semi-circular courts (*a, b*) through which, as through the three transverse parts (*c, d, e*), runs the main throughway with entrance at (*f*). Centrally, to the left, are two stairways that are arranged in two flights (*g*) with a passage between giving access to the long main building with the prince's apartments (*h*).Where the two arcs meet is a chapel (*i*) with three altars. The rest is so arranged that there is room enough throughout the three storeys for accommodating a great princely household. The façade springs from a raised *socle* with a massive facing of grooved masonry. The two upper storeys, however, are smooth and have windows flush with the façade. Since there is a chapel within this building a small tower is superimposed—and, for the sake of symmetry, another little tower on the long main block above the simple German roof.

Tab. III.

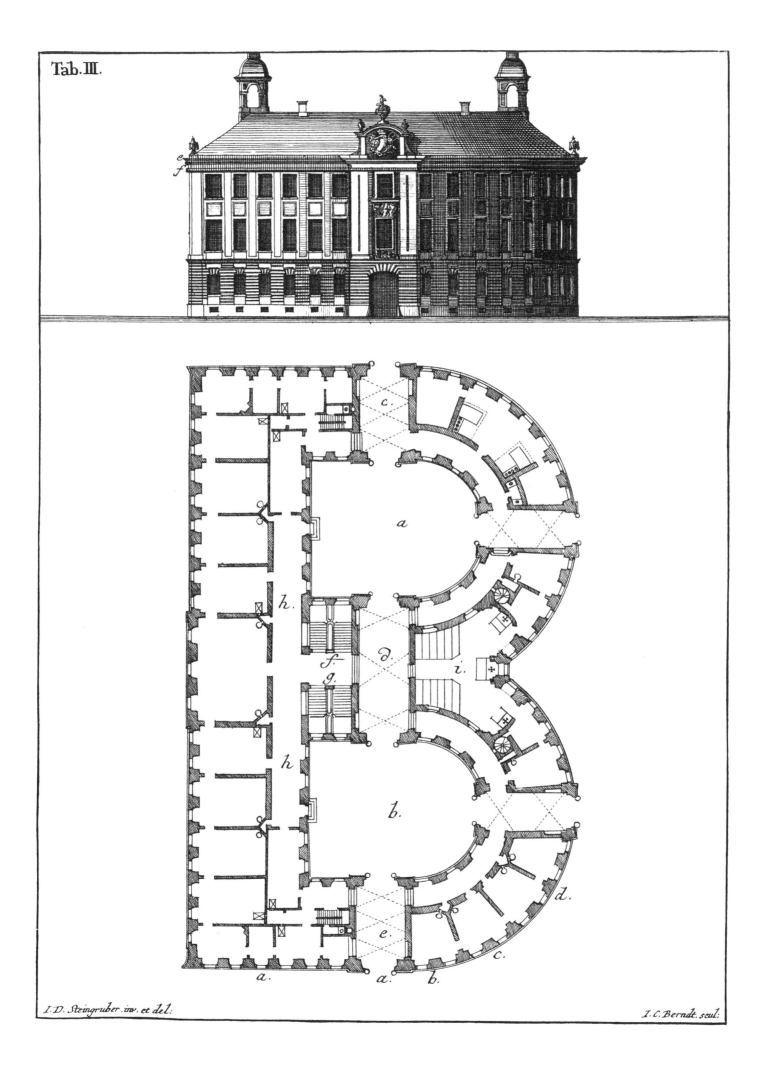

I.D. Steingruber inv. et del:

I.C. Berndt sculp:

V.D

ALTHOUGH one might indeed surmise that no building could be based on this letter-shape, one such plan is given so as to keep things in good order. Accordingly, (*a*) there is a reasonably large court, with the best, residential rooms in the long main arm of the building, as their lordships' apartments (*b, c, d, e*), with ⊙ indicating a great dining-room; and in the curved 'wing', (*f*) kitchen and (*g*) *Conditorei* [confectionery kitchen], and near by (*h, i*) guest chambers and various other rooms necessary to such an establishment. Stairways (*k, l*) next to the entrance gates, and easily overlooked. [*l* is not on engraving.] A spacious corridor (*m, n*) completely encircling the courtyard and linking various rooms. Heating arrangements and other conveniences are, as far as possible, inconspicuous. To right and left of the rear entry (*o*) are (*p, q*) two matching flights of stairs.

The elevation is rusticated and the upper *refends* set off with Greek capitals. For a change, we have here a mansard roof.

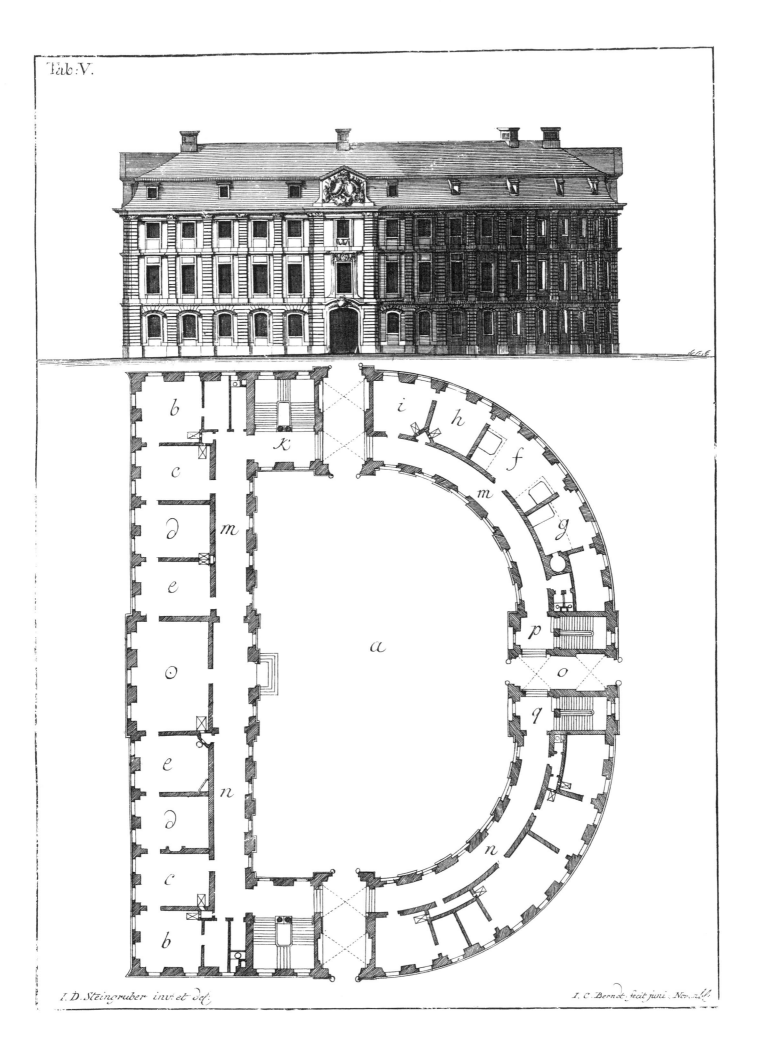

I. D. Steingruber inv. et del. I. C. Bernet fecit juni. Nor. 1.

VI.E

THIS letter is of fairly regular shape, but even so the main entrances (*a*) must be on the short arms, so that apartments (*b*, *c*) for their lordships, and the centrally placed, suitably large dining-hall (*d*) may be included in the long main range of buildings. In the upper cross-wing is the kitchen (*e*) adjoining rooms (*f*) for the staff; while in the lower wing is a *Salét'gen* (*g*) in the corresponding area. In the middle, characterizing the letter E, is a church (*h*). However, this could be replaced by a handsome main staircase and entry or a special *Salét'gen*.

The elevation is shown from the courtyard side, because of the church, which is covered by a dome. This façade stands on a raised *socle*, and Corinthian pilasters soar through the two lower floors; and an appropriately styled attic floor rises above them.

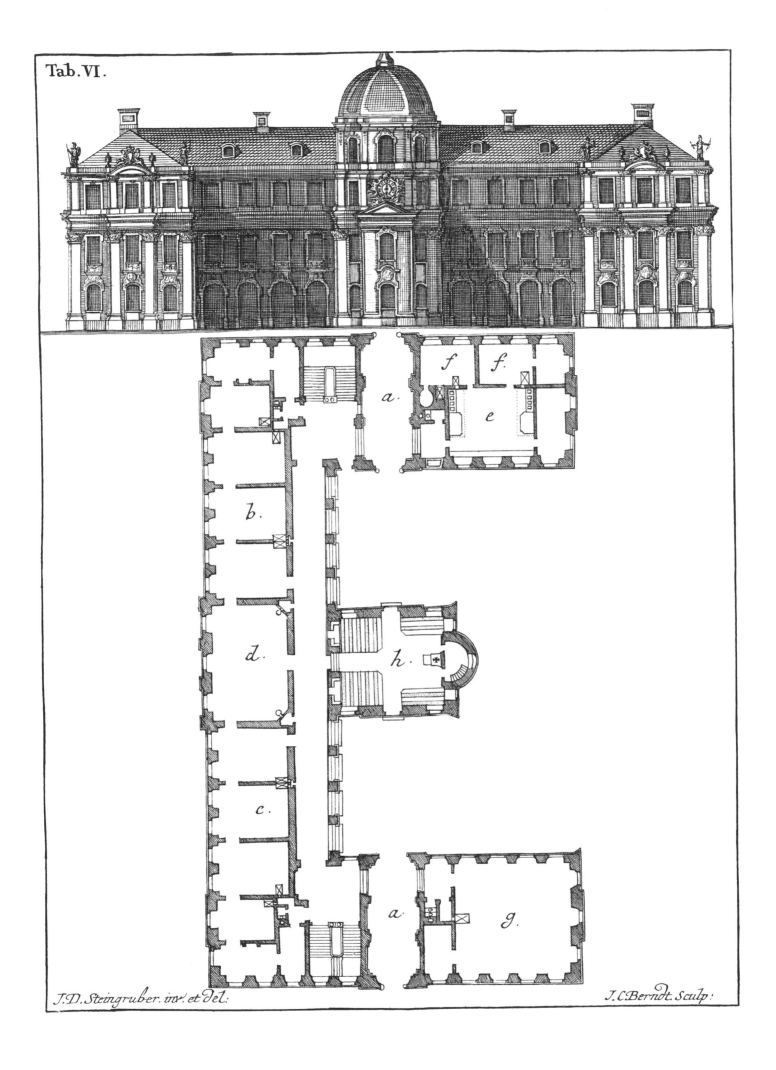

Tab. VI.

J.D. Steingruber. inv. et del:

J.C. Berndt. Sculp:

VII.F

IN the central arm of this form is, (*a*) the carriage-entrance, (*b*) a triple main stairway with one flight for ascent and two for descent. In the middle of the main edifice is (*c*) a large dining-hall, and on both sides of this (*d, e, f, g, h*) rooms for the lords' use. At the top, in the cross-wing, is (*i*) an anteroom, and adjoining it (*k*) the great hall.

Kitchens, cellars, and service rooms generally may be located in the *souterrain*, as there is a raised *socle*.

The façade is built up with double *refends* on the ground floor, paired Ionic pilasters on the second, and an attic storey at the top.

Tab. VII.

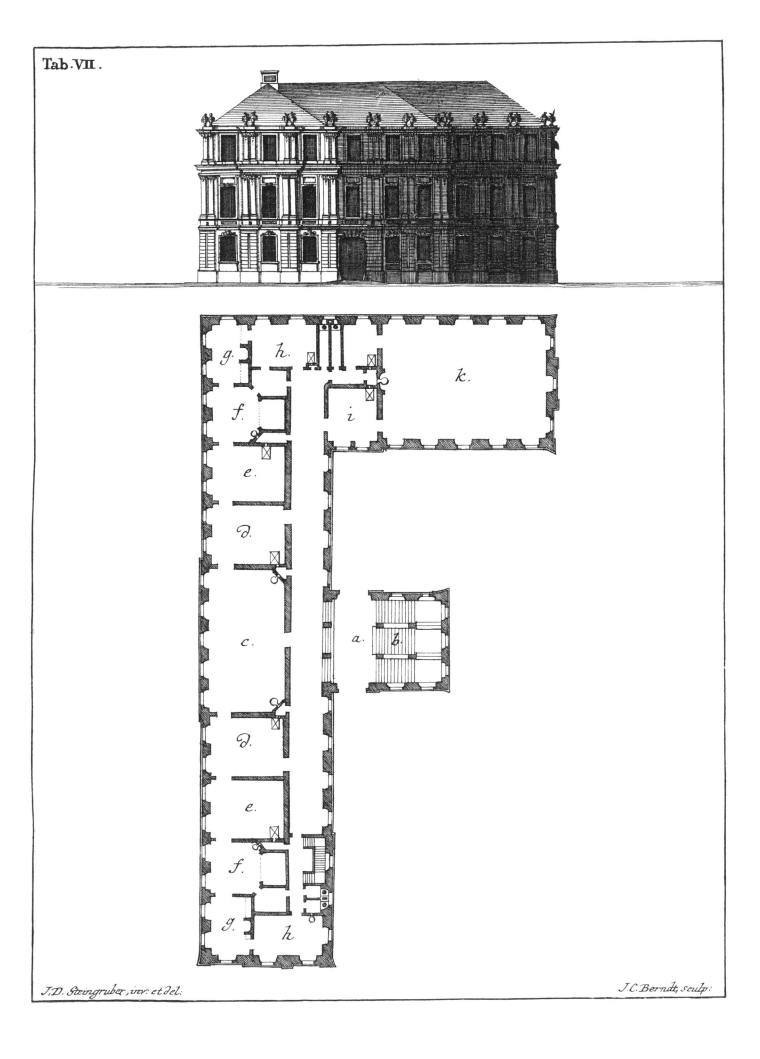

J.D. Steingruber, inv. et del: J.C. Berndt, sculp:

VIII . G

THE G again presents a form not easily adaptable to an architectural plan, although there is a possibility of basing thereon a residence for personages of rank and their exalted guests. Close to the main entry (*a*) are wide and commodious flights of stairs (*b, c*) with nine rooms on one side (*d*) and seven on the other (*e*). Next to the second of these is the great hall (*f*). All the rooms, if we except one or two *cabinets*, which have fireplaces, could be heated from the corridor, so that none of their lordships need be disturbed or inconvenienced. The usual offices would be, as usual, in the *souterrain*. The façade is of no particular architectural order, since between their *refends* the windows are set off with recessed plaques bearing carved escutcheons, bas-reliefs, and so on, those on the middle floor with masks and those on the upper floor with garlands in the Attic style; elements of this nature make an effective show on buildings such as this.

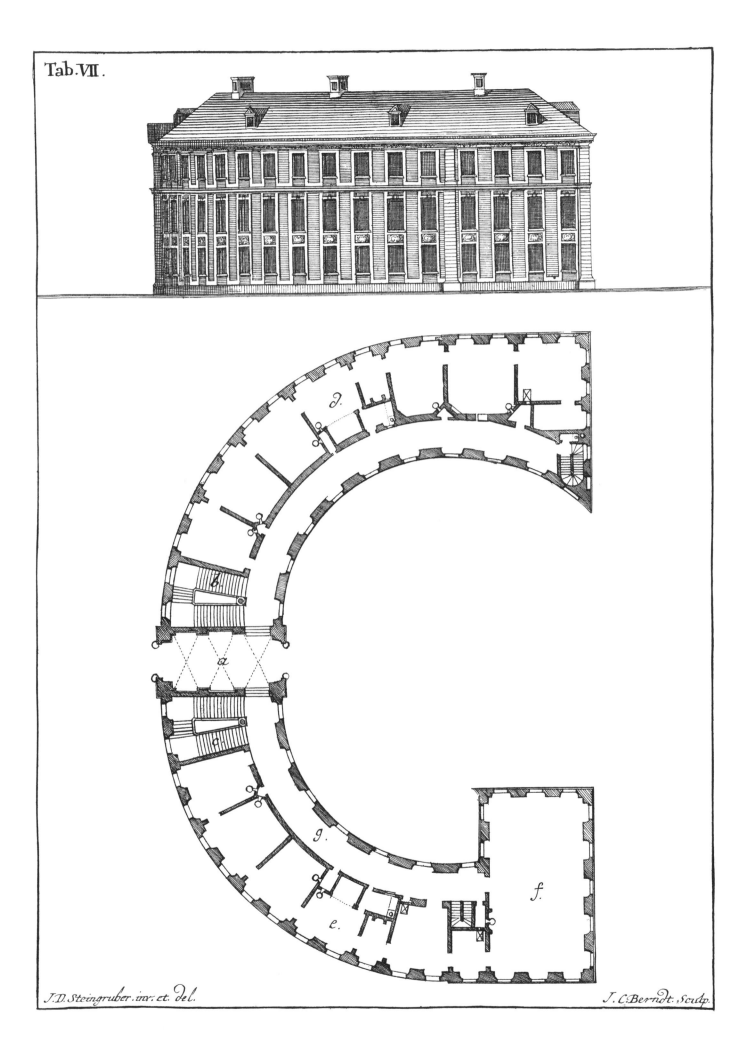

Tab. VII.

J.D. Steingruber. inv. et. del.

J. C. Berndt. Sculp.

IX.H

THIS letter is so balanced in form that it lends itself admirably to a design for a palace in the country for a personage of consequence, especially if the layout allows for two small *parterres* beyond the main entry, between the two long wings, to supplement the great park. The octagonal pavilion (*a*) set in the centre could furnish a small but by no means negligible *salon* reached by way of adjoining flights of stairs (*b*) leading also to the two long wings. The ordinary dining-room [as distinct from the ceremonial] is located centrally (*c*) and to right and left are (*d, e*) their lordships' apartments. And since the building has three storeys, and a *Mezane* above the lowest for the domestic staff, and since the various service rooms are in the *souterrain*, a royal court could be accommodated. The concealed stairs [*f* in engraving, omitted from text], heating arrangements and other conveniences are so arranged as to spare the distinguished household any inconvenience.

The lowest floor of the façade is in the Tuscan rustic mode, the other two, taking in the pavilion, have half-columns, and the side buildings Ionic pilasters. A balustrade adorned with statues and vases conceals the roof.

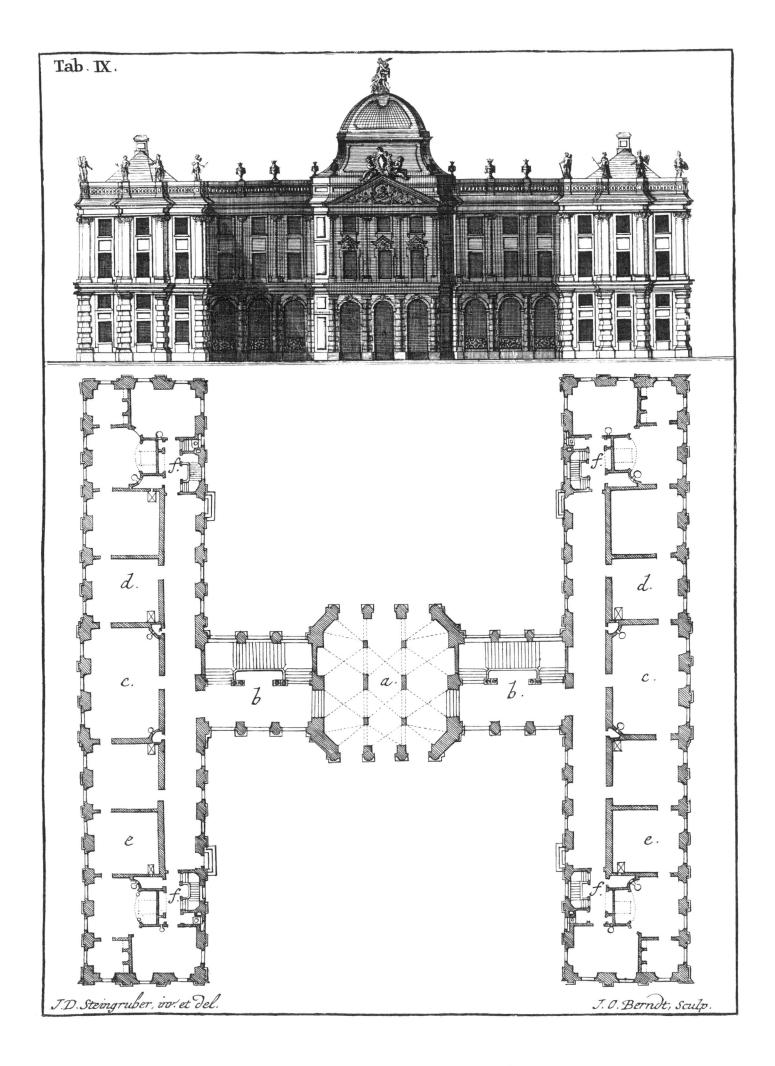

Tab. IX.

a. *b.* *c.* *d.* *e.* *f.*

J. D. Steingruber, inv. et del.   J. O. Berndt, Sculp.

X . I

I T is all too simple to draw this figure in elevation, so I have permitted myself the conceit of adding a small E to one side of it and a small A to the other, thus representing 'E I A', a word expressing jubilation. In the middle of the I we have (*a*) church and cloister, and (*b, c, d, e, f, g*) twelve cells for monks and, behind these, quarters for the Superior (*h, i, k, l*). Beyond his quarters is (*m*) a large refectory. Cellar, kitchen, and so on to be in the *souterrain*, so that in the two side buildings could be necessary offices connected with the monastic economy. (*n, o*) Courtyards, and, to right and left, (*p, q*) two little gardens, with, in the centre, (*r, s*) ponds.

Admittedly, in view of the threefold nature of the building, this is a somewhat forced solution, serving only to fill out a page and demonstrate to what lengths architectural notions may be taken.

The front elevation of main and minor buildings is in Doric style with an Ionic attic storey, and the church has an imposing cupola. The side buildings are quite simply designed.

Tab: X.

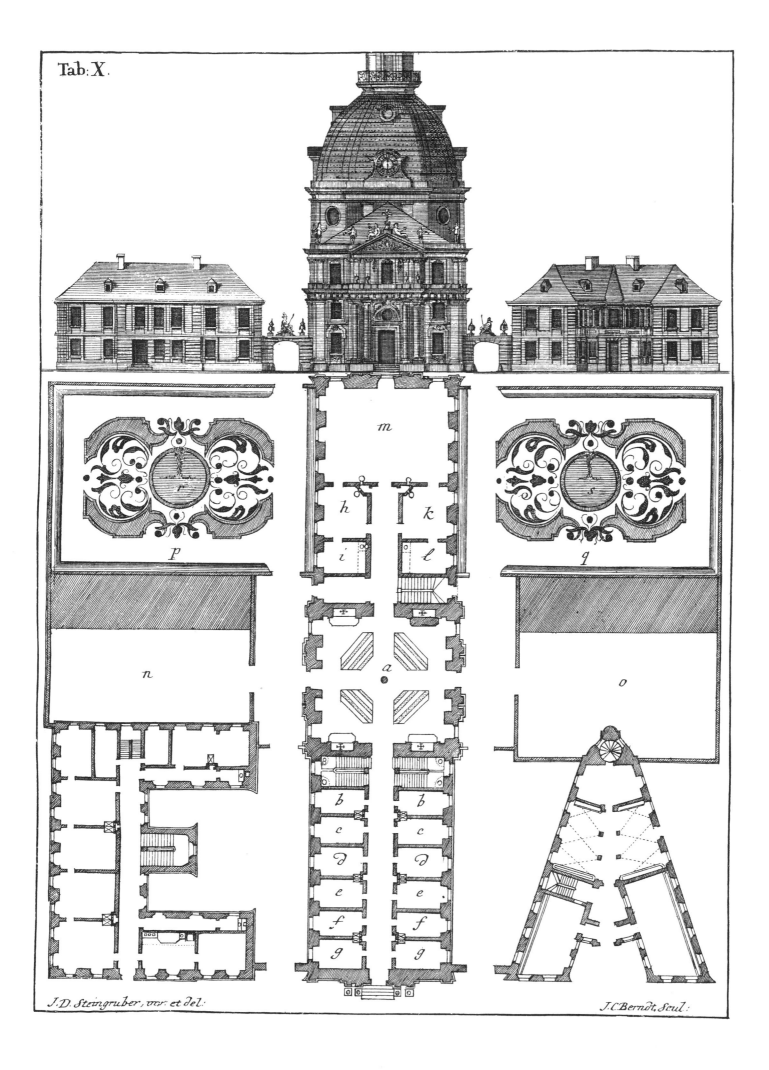

J.D. Steingruber, inv: et del: J.C.Berndt, Scul:

XI . K

HERE again is a letter of such a form that the amateur prepared to base a palace upon it would be hard to find. Yet, as the arrangement shows, a great household could be accommodated in reasonable style. And though the building must be long [in proportion to its width] in order to retain the letter-shape, yet with the division into rooms fairly uniform, there is nevertheless ample scope for introducing change and variation here and there.

In the centre is (a) a spacious hall, and on both sides—above (b, c, d, e, f) and below (g, h, i, k, l)—the private apartments; beyond these, on the courtyard side, concealed staircase and closet, and adjoining them, the heating arrangement. To the right hand of the through passage (m), and at the junction of the two outer curves, is (n) the main staircase. And, to be sure, a design of this nature is by no means unpleasing. To the left, (o) the entry to (p) [this is marked o on the engraving. The error persists as far as x, and v is missing. For the sake of clarity, this description will follow the letters on the engraving]—the long corridor giving access to above-mentioned rooms. To the right, in the rear courtyard (p) of the wing are (q) the main kitchen and (r) bakehouse, together with (s, t, u, w) the rest of the service rooms. In the lower courtyard of the other wing is (y) a *Salét'gen*, adjoined by two apartments (x and z) and a *cabinet* [note that x is wrongly marked].

The lowest storey of the façade is faced with rectangular freestone blocks, the two upper storeys with *refends* beyond the wings; and (implying the presence of gardens on both sides) garden walls decorated with statues.

Tab: XI.

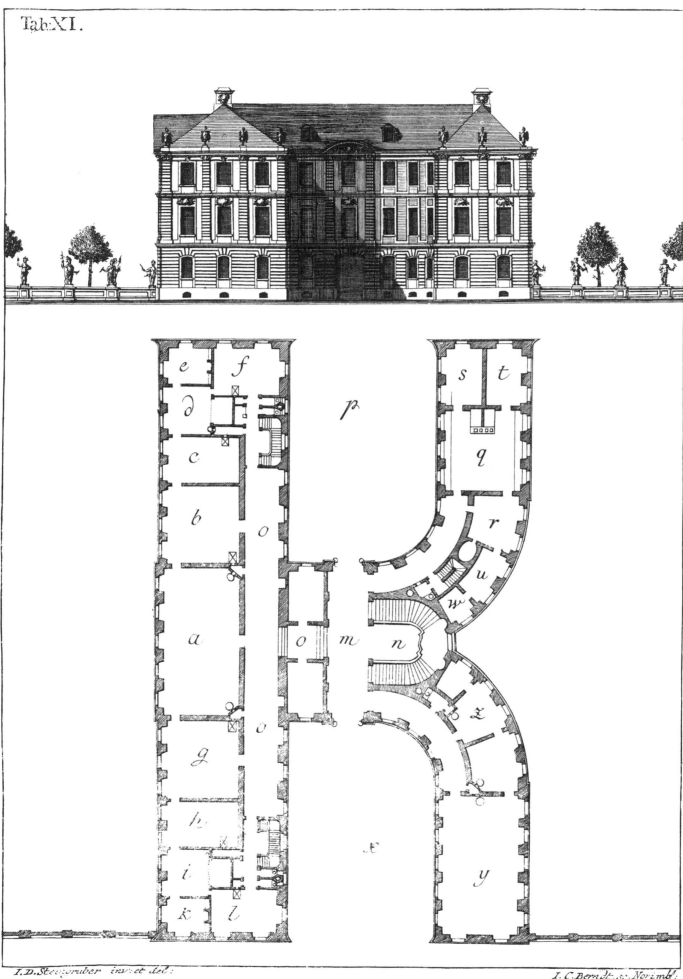

I.D.Steingruber inv. et del: I.C.Berndt sc. Norimb.

XIV. SECOND M

SINCE this letter occurs so often when the names of personages of rank are set down, and since its characteristics, proportions, and contours can vary, another interpretation is given here. It is indeed true that the layout of the two main wings is almost exactly the same as in the preceding plan, but the central section has a totally different aspect on account of (*a*) [omitted from plate] the achievement of a far from unpleasing effect by a large oblong hall (over which a handsome *salon* might be built) by the addition of free-standing columns on each side, with statues or groups of statuary in the niches between them. Moreover, there are main staircases of various kinds, one of these (*b*) in a half-circle, and having either very shallow treads or a ramp for riding or conveying; another one (*c*) arranged in three flights.

The plan is such that there is no difficulty about carrying it out for some great personage—as the gentle reader interested in architecture will readily concede.

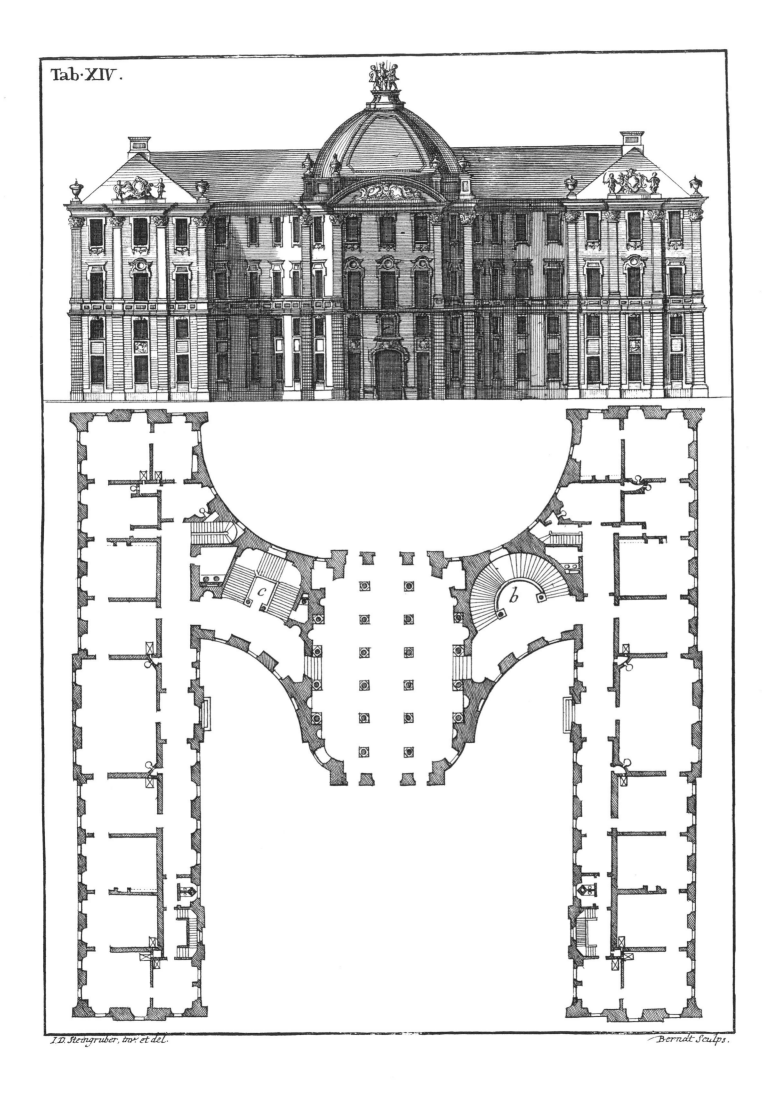

Tab·XIV.

c

b

I.D.Steingruber, inv. et del.

Berndt Sculps.

XV . N

BUT building according to this figure could lead to a very awkward arrangement, since laying it out without blurring the letter-form is indeed difficult, with all to be heated by stoves or some other means. Here we have (*a*) the carriage-way, an oblong octagon with paired columns supporting the main hall above. Ascending from the vestibule to right and left are fine-looking stairways with landings (*b*, *c*), and closets are concealed near by. Thence, by way of an irregular passage and (*d*) the main corridor, to the main wing, with dining-room and private apartments. Access thereto is also possible from the courtyards through the two (*e*) arches, leading to (*d*) the truncated main corridor, with lesser stairs and closets fitted in. By these various means the characteristic shape of the letter is well enough represented.

The façade shows a mezzanine floor and facing of grooved ashlar blocks. Ionic pilasters rise through the two upper storeys; the great hall and pavilion are roofed over with a cupola surmounted by a railed-in platform.

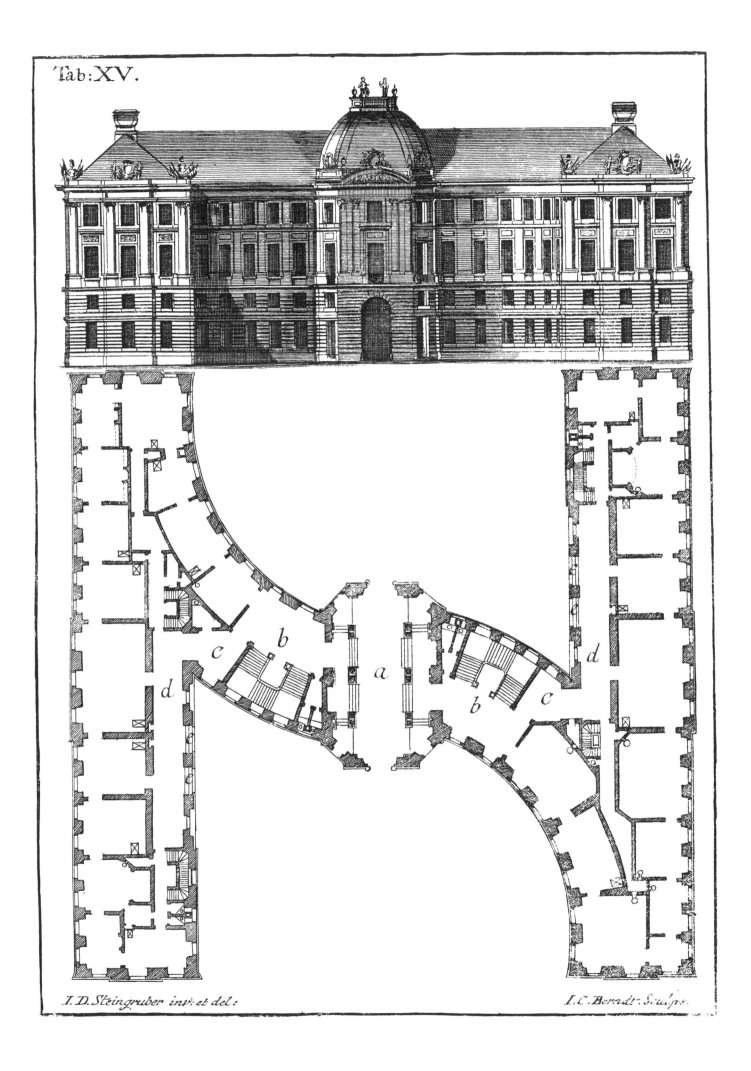

Tab: XV.

I.D. Steingruber inv: et del: *I.C. Berndt. Sculps.*

XVI.O

THE letter O is here given a somewhat oval form, and although the rounded contours result in rooms of slightly irregular shape, yet four persons of rank could be comfortably housed with appropriate *logis,* and each in privacy thanks to (*1, 2, 3, 4*) different staircases. And with (*5*) the front and (*6*) the back entries sufficing, then (*7, 8*) the two great vestibules to right and left could be flanked on both sides by gardens (*9, 10, 11, 12*). On the two lower storeys the summer *Salét'gen,* and the great hall above occupying the top storey and the whole height of the cupola; then kitchens, *Conditorey* and other service rooms would be in the *souterrain.*

Because of the rounded shape the façade is quite plain in design, with cupolas crowned with groups of sculpture over the two great *salons.*

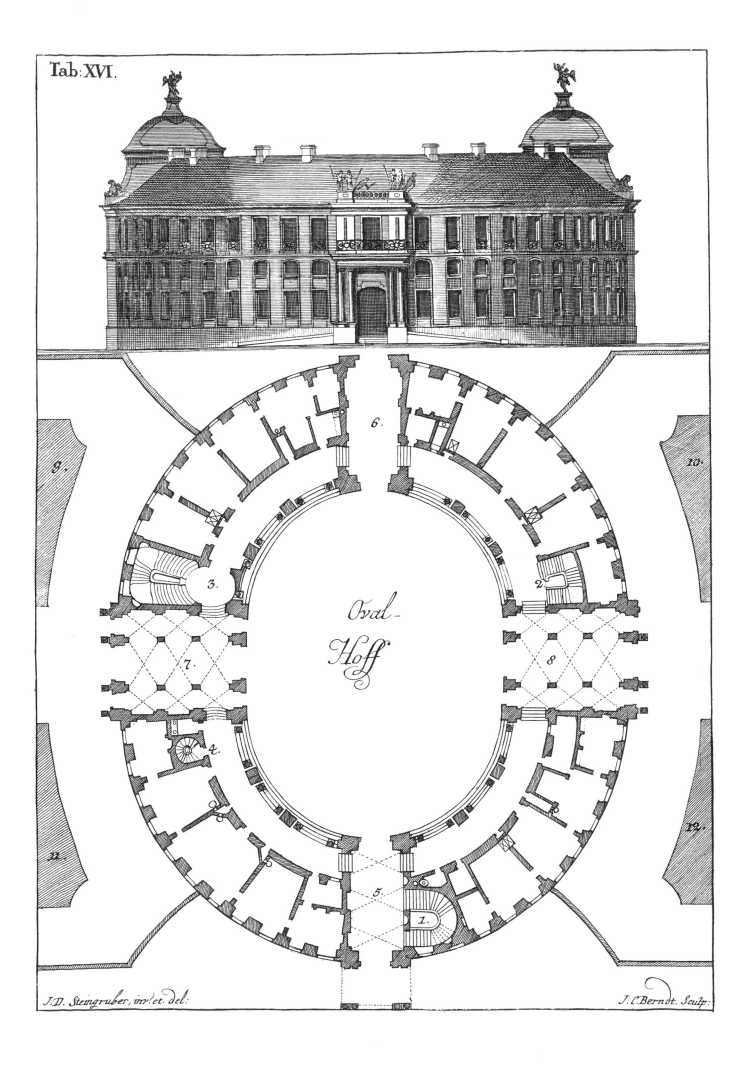

Tab: XVI.

Oval-
Hoff

J.D. Steingruber, inv: et. del:

J.C.Berndt. Sculp:

XVII . P

ALTHOUGH we have delineated this letter on the same measure as, and in proportion with, preceding ones, and of the same height, it still proves to be the smallest, apart from I. Yet it can be utilized in such a way that a noble lord could be suitably housed, and with all possible convenience, especially with the kitchen premises located in the upper rounded area, so that, with earlier plans to go by, there are no further observations that need to be made.

The elevation shows the mezzanine set in arches, but the upper floors are plain, the angles of the building with *refends*; and the roof is *à la Mansarde*.

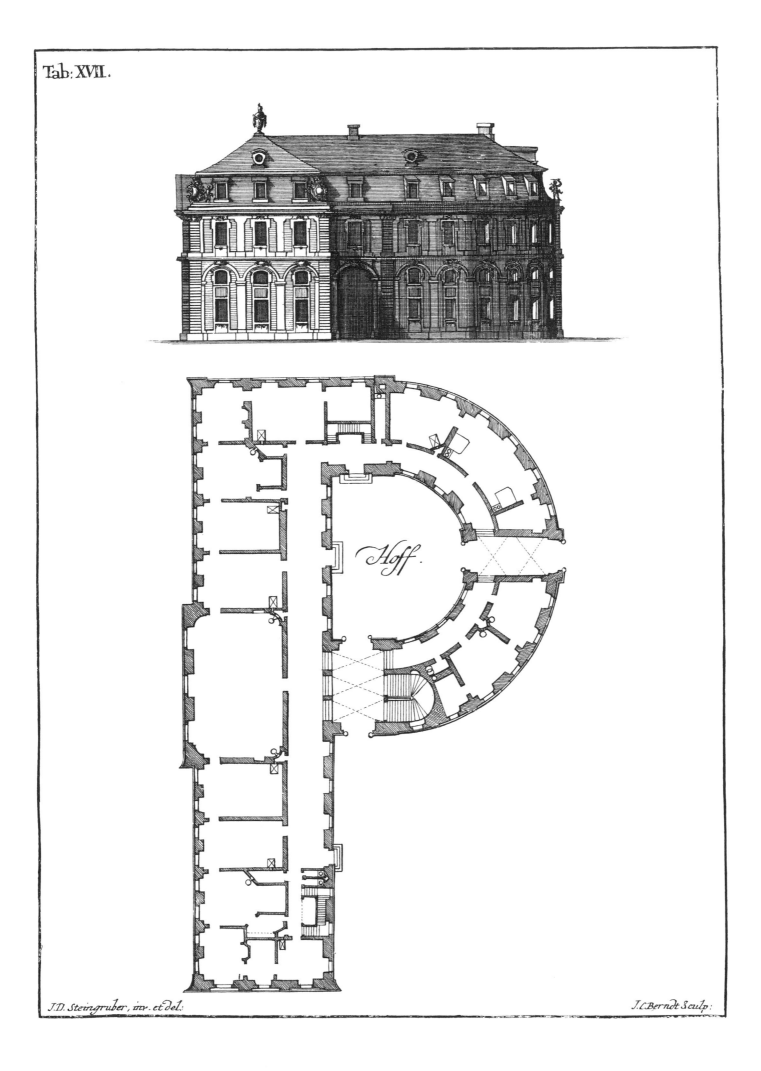

Hoff.

J.D. Steingruber, inv. et del: J.C. Berndt Sculp:

XVIII & XIX . Q

THE feature of this letter, its tail, of course presents certain difficulties if we are to refrain from flouting the rules laid down. And the solution is to envisage a site on a mountainside or hill-slope. Then on one side is (*a*) the entrance at the foot of the incline, and by way of a slightly curved (*b*) through-passage, a gentle upward gradient, with an outlet half-way up by way of (*c*) a winding flight of steps, and in addition, (*d*) a stairway in two flights, both leading up to the first floor. (*e*) Kitchens and (*f*) bakehouses and cellars are in the basement.

The first storey in the spacious oval courtyard stands on a raised *socle* in the second plan, which makes for such ease, such comfortable accommodation, that a royal court could reside here. Above the entry, in this case, is a small garden, clearly emphasizing the characteristic tail in this second plan. And in order to fit the building more neatly into the oval, on the side opposite the entry is a sham doorway—and if, alongside this raised terrace, gardens are laid out on both sides, an orangery could be arranged below. And this, with the three storeys as shown in the sketch [xviii] with a gallery, would give this mountain castle a magnificent exterior; and together with the mansard roof would ensure more light and air on the courtyard side, as suggested in the cross-section of the elevation.

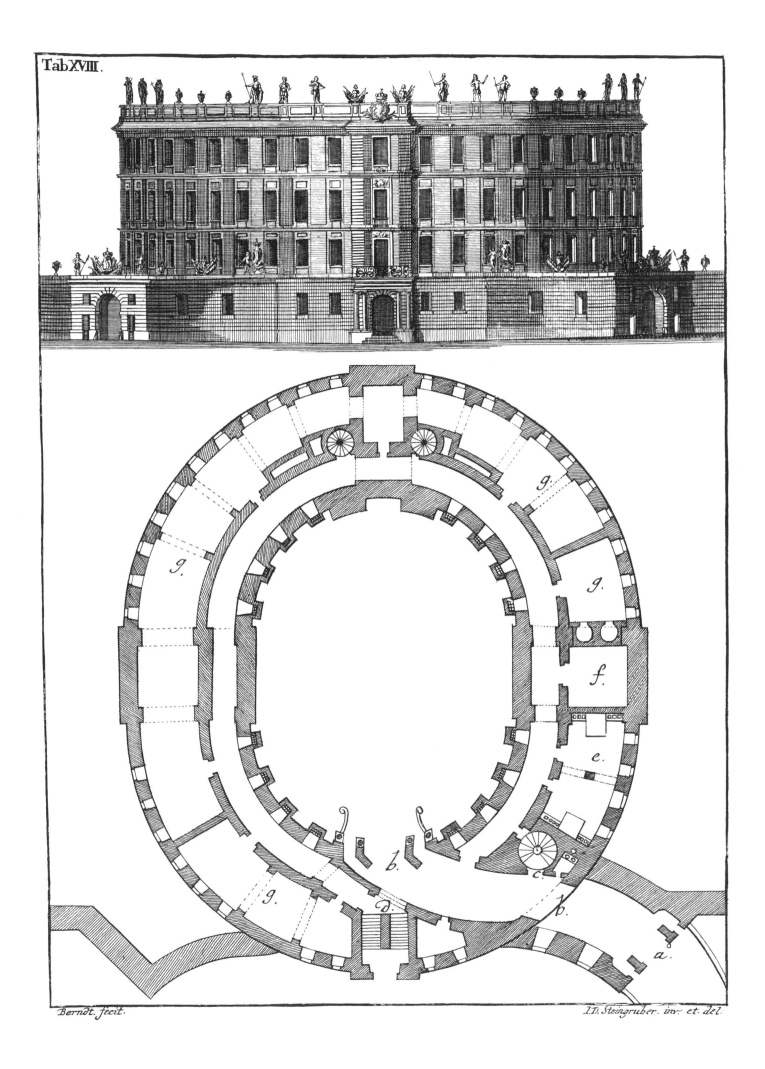

Tab. XVIII.

Berndt. fecit.

I.D. Steingruber. inv. et. del.

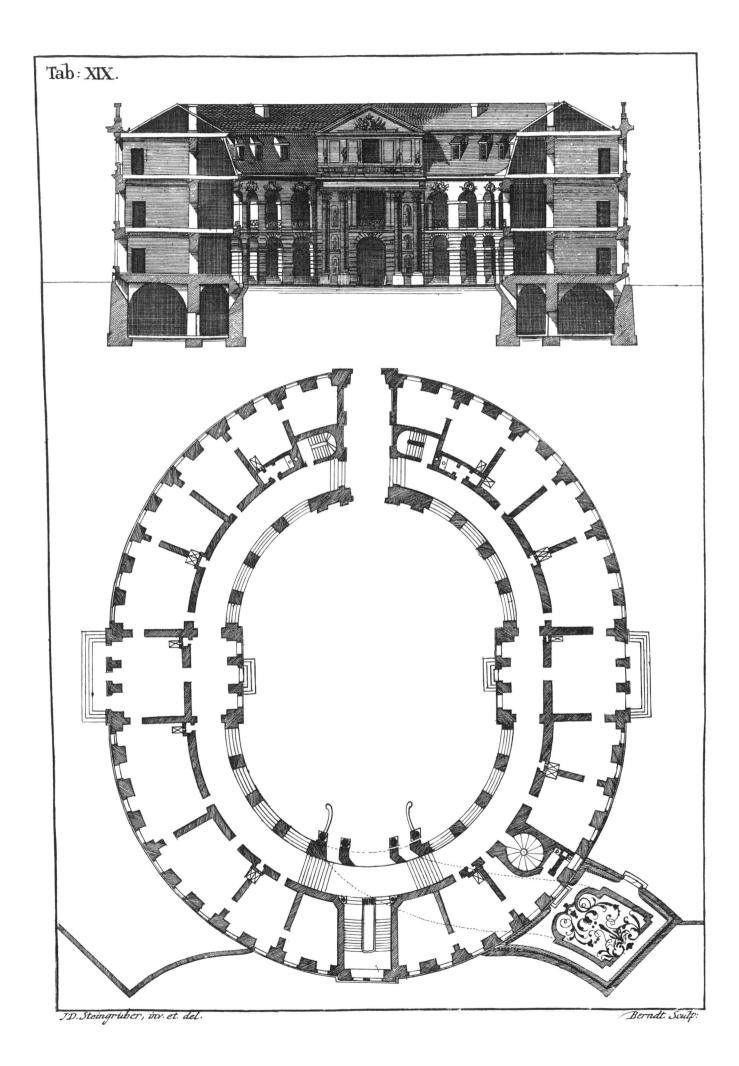

Tab: XIX.

J.D. Steingruber, inv. et. del.

Berndt Sculp:

XX . R

As characteristics of letters vary so much, so must the buildings based on them vary, especially in the divisions of internal space. Even though the main long arm in this letter shows no notable differences, the disposition of rooms allows for commodious private apartments on both sides of the main hall.

The upper curve, with the crossbar, encloses a small courtyard, but another similar courtyard below has more open access at the entry. In (*a*) the carriage-way is (*b*) a double stairway arranged in five flights, the middle one leading from the *sou-bassement* to the first floor; and the other two, as well as the middle one, giving access to higher floors.

To the right, where the two curves meet, is (*c*) the palace chapel, with three altars, and on the upper side of this (*d*) a priest's lodging; below, (*e*) the sacristy, and in the wing below, (*f*) another small hall; and adjoining this, (*g, h*) two further chambers. In the upper curve, (*i*) the kitchen and (*k, l*) the larders are located.

As already mentioned, this edifice has a *sou-bassement* and three storeys above it; and since there is a place of worship within the building there is a bell and clock-tower above it.

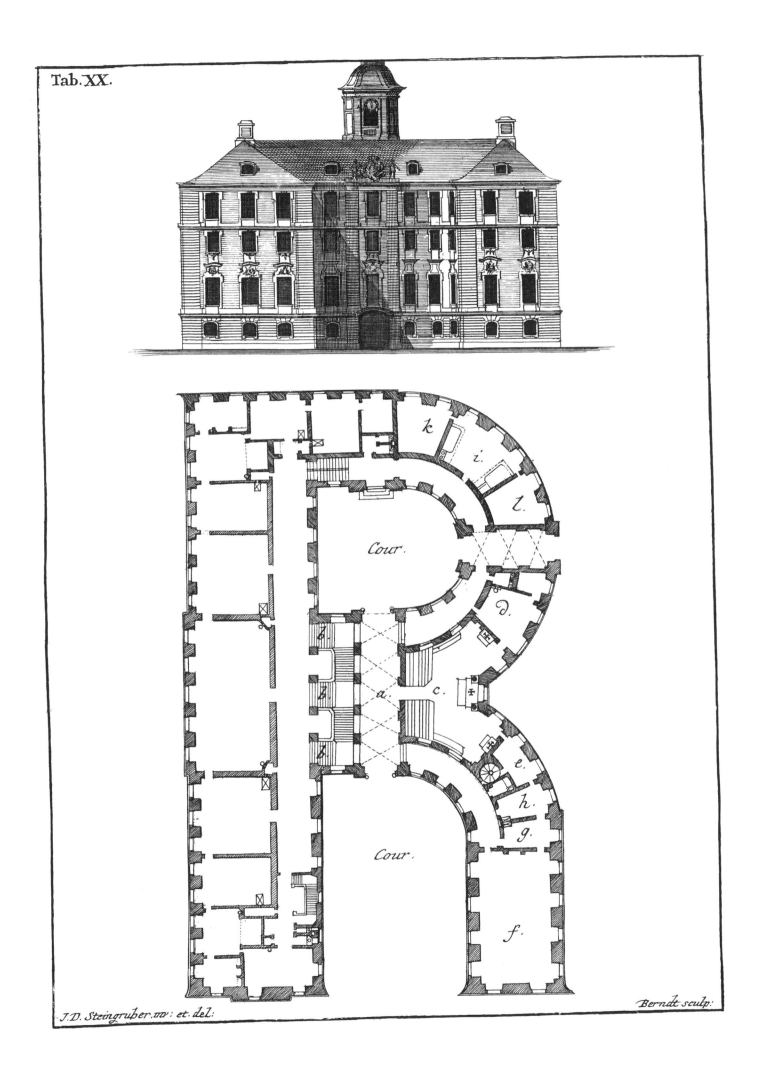

Tab. XX.

Cour.

Cour.

k
i.
l.
d.
c.
e.
h.
g.
f.
a.

J.D. Steingruber. inv: et. del:

Berndt sculp:

XXI. SECOND R

ALTHOUGH, all things considered, it may indeed be difficult to arrange buildings of the required kind in conformity with such letter-forms, yet the main task in all these designs is to make the best use in every case of the spaces available while still bringing to the main prospect as high a degree of symmetry as possible. Therefore, in the preceding plan one side wing is somewhat narrower than the main block and has only two windows instead of three. By way of compensation, the rest of the side wing and the front of the main block are brought into symmetry by providing three windows to make the two widths equal; and the rest is narrowed towards the back of the curve. The divisions of the main block correspond for the most part with those already described in the preceding account, but the main stairs and domestic chapel are differently disposed, and the façades are different in design.

Tab. XXI.

J.D. Steingruber, inv. et del:

Berndt sculp

XXII.S

To erect a building according to this letter-form is to create, as none will gainsay, a curiosity rather than a workable building. Even so, disposed thus: from (*a*) to (*i*) and from (*k*) to (*s*), [*r* and *s* are omitted from plate] there is scope for a royal residence with, from *1* to *12*, room enough for the servants. One drawback is that *A* and *B*, the two circular *Salét'gen*, are somewhat small, yet they are freely accessible by way of curved and straight passages and the two principal and four spiral stairways—so arranged that with no trespass on the private apartments there is free communication with no one person impeding another.

Kitchens and other necessary offices are on the ground floor, but other service rooms and heating arrangements are as far as possible kept inconspicuous.

The elevation shows a solidly constructed ground floor, but the upper storeys have soaring Ionic pilasters, their straight sides decorated with single, their rounded sides with double, pilaster strips; above them is a gallery with statues and vases, and a group in Italianate style surmounts the tower.

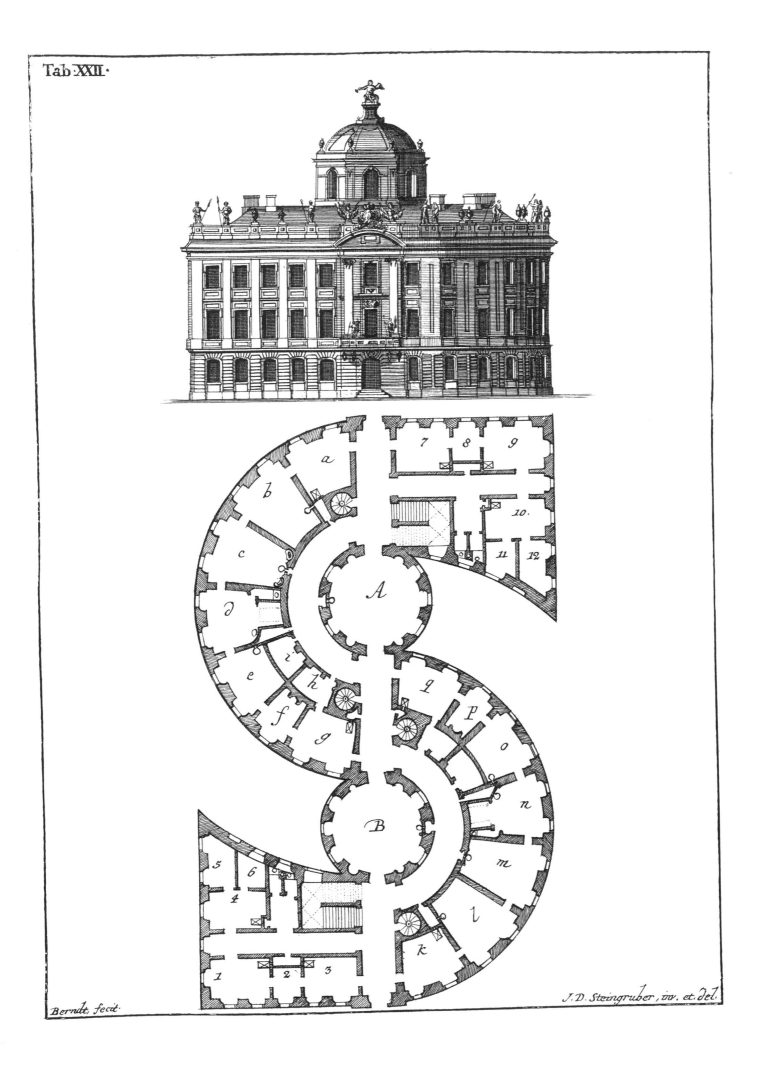

Berndt, fecit.

J.D. Steingruber, inv. et del.

XXIII . T

THIS figure again leads to something that is diverting, with scope for all kinds of notions. Yet it is pre-eminently a case where the letter-form can be most distinctly represented—whereas, in many preceding examples, and in some yet to come, the layout needs to be viewed from a height or from the top of a tower if the letter is to be clearly recognizable.

Since there is nothing remarkable about the allocation of space, no further explanation is called for.

The two lower storeys of the façade are massively constructed and with *refends*, but the two upper storeys are in the new Goldmann* style, with straight pilaster strips on the sides, and term statuary between. The roof is *à la Mansarde*.

* Probably a reference to Nicolaus Goldmann (1623–65) whose influence
was still felt many years after his death.

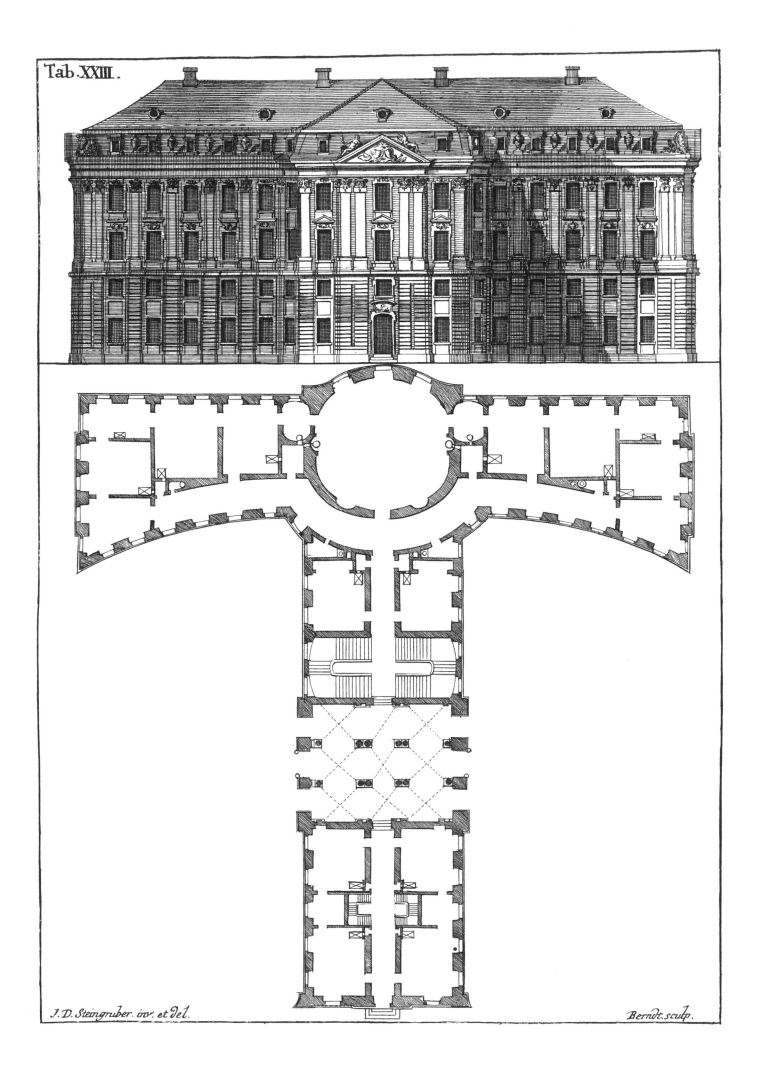

Tab. XXIII.

J.D. Steingruber. inv. et del.

Berndt. sculp.

XXIV . U

ON the other hand, this letter is of a shape entirely appropriate for a palace design, permitting of a handsome courtyard and two long wings with ample apartments, and a lower transverse block comprising two *salons*, one built above the other, with *cabinets* on each side adjoining two small galleries, and beyond these, by way of the courtyard and through two separate gateways, magnificent stairways having either one or two approaches, but at all events two outlets.

The elevation shows a lower storey with single pilasters and an upper one, that of the state rooms, with Corinthian pilasters; but all with plain and proportionate pilaster strips.

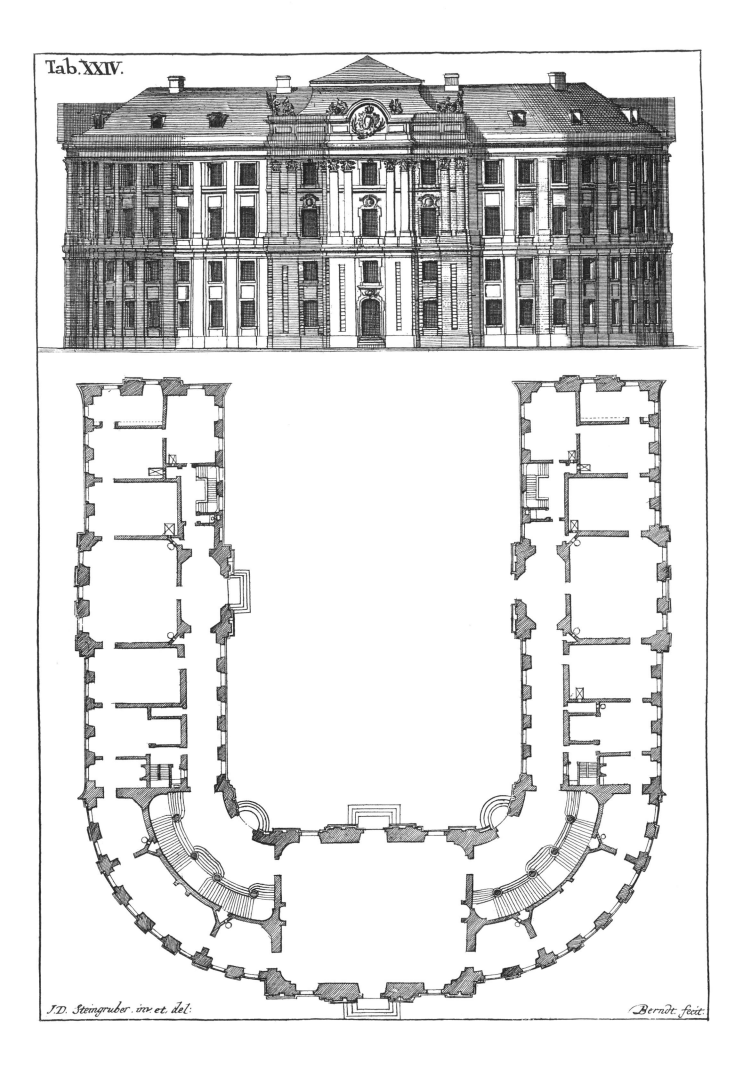

Tab. XXIV.

J.D. Steingruber. inv. et. del:

Berndt. fecit:

XXV.V

HERE again, adherence to the letter-form results in a contrived effect; however, the present arrangement shows the two long wings divided much as in the preceding plan, save that with this letter the lower part lends itself to a large vestibule shaped within two semi-circular walls with recesses; above this vestibule, in the two upper storeys, is a splendid great hall with vaulted ceiling that ascends right into the roof space. On all floors are staircases and corridors leading to the various rooms.

The two lower storeys are faced with grooved masonry blocks. Ionic columns run through the full height of the projecting façade of the two upper storeys with perpendicular panels and strips between them. A roof *à la Mansarde* covers the building.

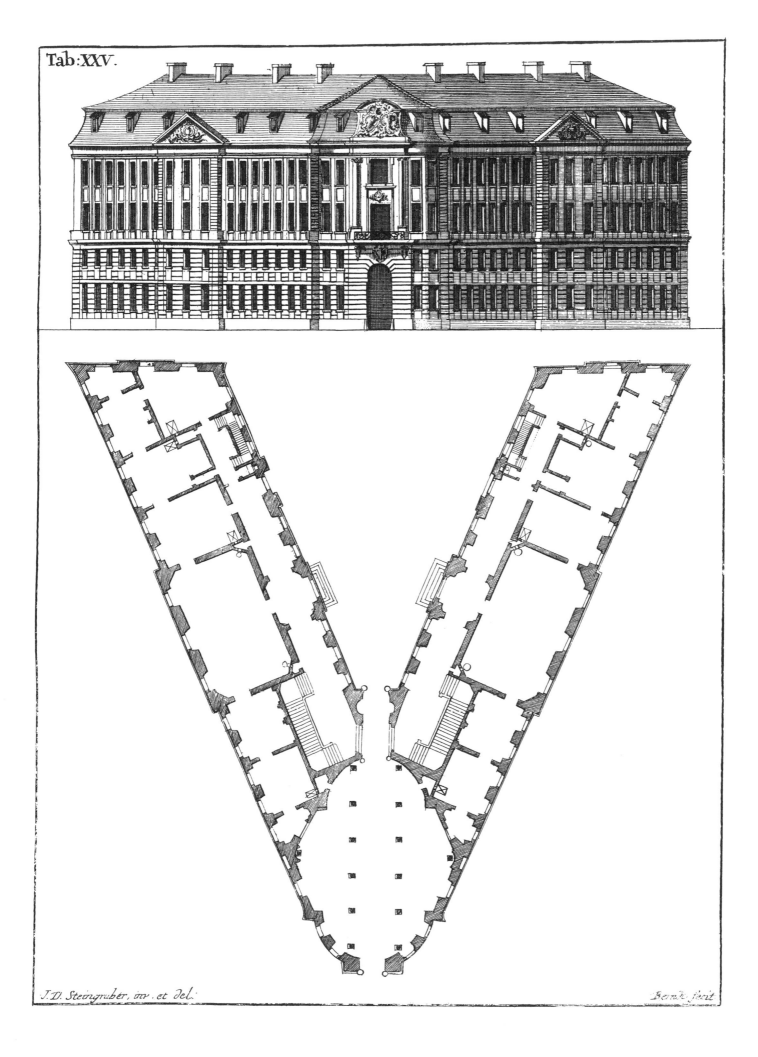

Tab:XXV.

XXVI. W

IT might well be conjectured that no really acceptable building, no really suitable accommodation, could be based on this letter-form, yet in the end a workable idea emerged, with the W shape by no means unrecognizable.

This idea presumes an entry forecourt laid out at the lower end, sixty feet wide and fifty feet deep; beyond this entry a rectangular vestibule leads to an oval reception hall. To right and left between this vestibule and hall the two principal stairways are so arranged that I, for my part, have never seen anything to match them, either on paper or *in natura*. On the landings half-way up these flights are ornamental sculptured groups, and as there are three landings in all, the stairs are easily negotiated. Imparting an original twist to the plan, there are two oval *cabinets* of adequate size at the two lower points of the W, and in the corridor behind each of these, on the forecourt side, two small rooms of irregular shape for servants. The heating arrangement is so situated as to be capable of warming two or three rooms from one system. As usual, the two long wings are reserved for private apartments; the detail thereof, and of the façade, being left to the individual choice of lovers and practitioners of the architectural art. And if any one of these is inclined to improve on my ideas I shall be glad to profit therefrom, since from time immemorial all sciences and arts have, from humble beginnings, developed and reached new levels of perfection, particularly the builder's art, lowly enough in its early days, as was pointed out in the preamble, yet now so lofty an art that there remains scarcely any room for further progress.

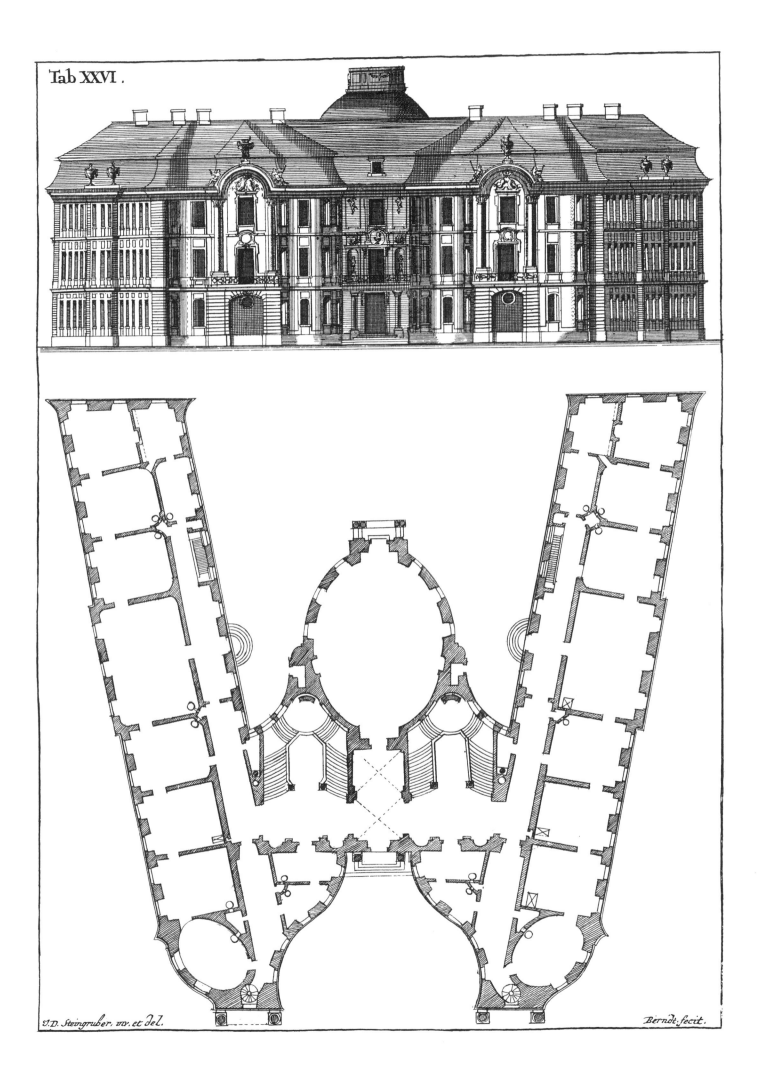

Tab XXVI.

J.D. Steingruber inv. et del.

Berndt fecit.

XXVII.X

As none will deny, both ecclesiastical and secular buildings have been based on the Cross of St Andrew, so no claims for a new invention are made here. Even so, this eminently secular building, laid out so as to comprise four spacious ranges of apartments, each with its own staircase and corridor leading to the centrally-located great hall, is worthy of benevolent consideration.

Corinthian columns rise through the two storeys of the façade. Encircled by the four roofs of the wings, and surmounting the hall, is a further storey, this time *all'italiana* and roofed over with a stepped dome.

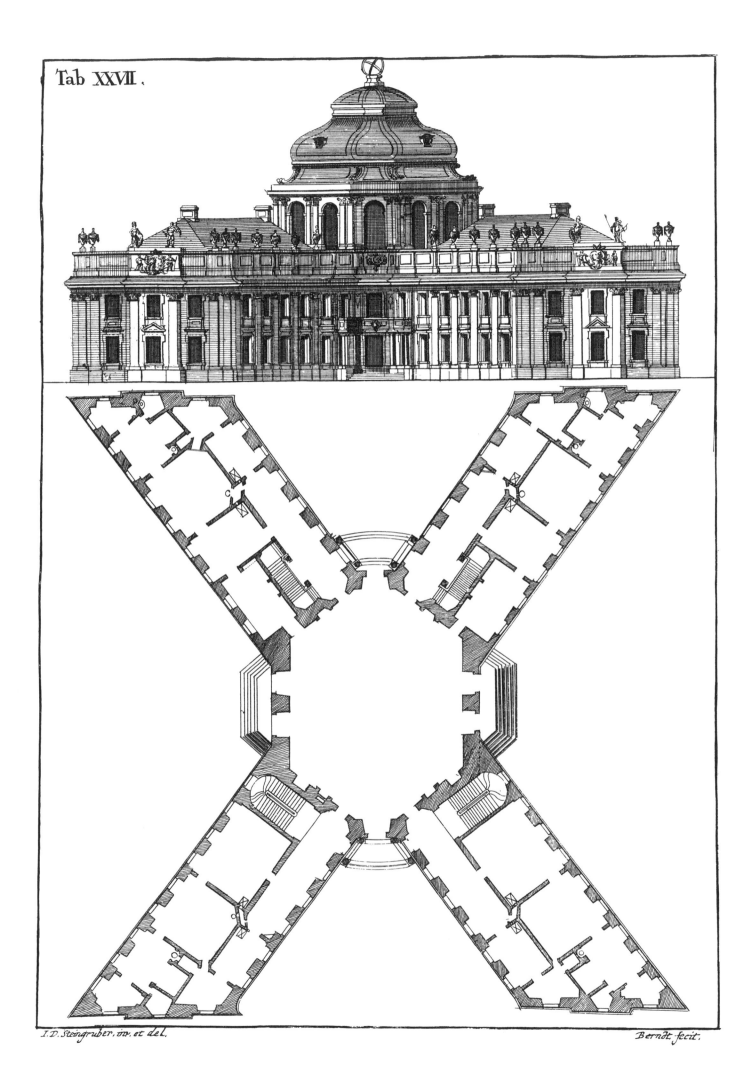

Tab XXVII.

I.D. Steingruber. inv. et del.

Berndt. fecit.

XXVIII. SECOND X

THE description for the preceding Letter X mentions the flights of stairs—these of two kinds, in one half-section with access to and from the great hall quite independent of the wings containing the private rooms, but in the other half with further access by stairway to a *cabinet*. In the second plan for X, since the central hall has a kind of double vestibule at both top and bottom through which, in symmetrical fashion, there is direct and uninterrupted communication between the four corridors and the apartments, just as many personages can be furnished with comfortable residence in the four wings.

As a variation on the first plan, the cupola is of a different design.

Tab. XVIII.

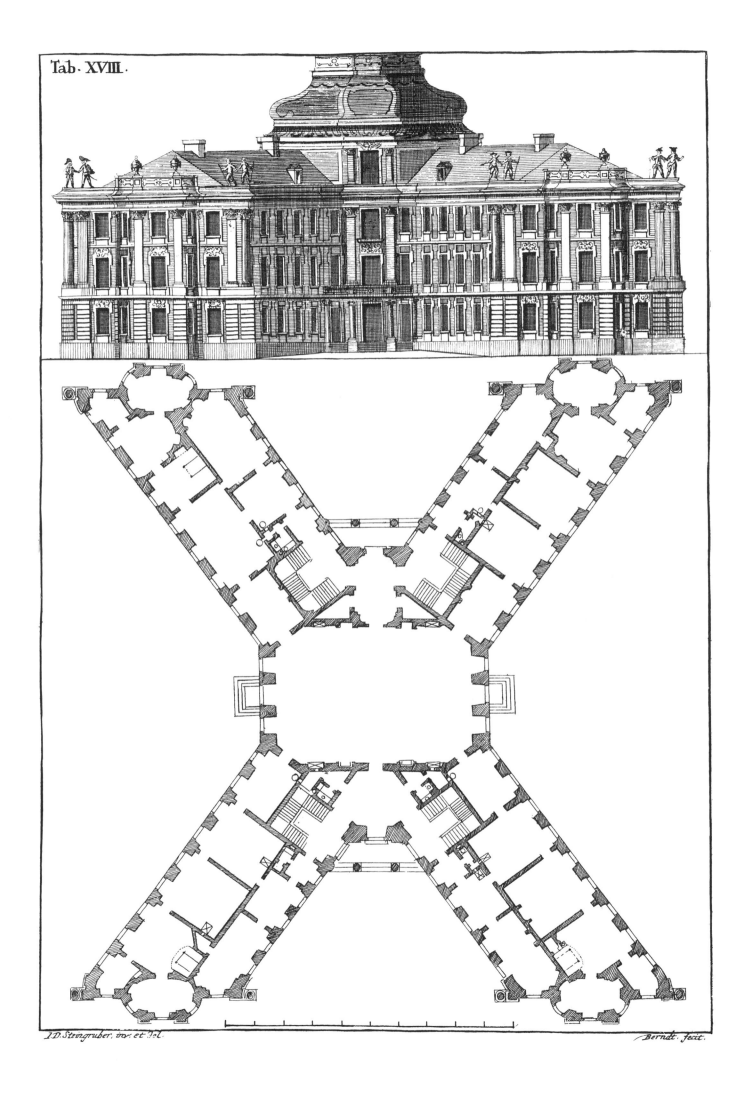

J.D.Steingruber, inv. et del.   Berndt. fecit.

XXIX . Y

DESIGNING on this letter-form is again a matter of producing some kind of edifice on a given pattern. Even though there is space enough, suitably divided, to accommodate personages of quality, the intersection of the three wings presents several problems. Yet the area of intersection may be utilized as a basically oblong-hexagonal main hall, from the two most important sides of which, as well as from the angle at the junction of the two upper wings, there will be sufficient view and sufficient daylight.

The front elevation shows a central uncovered flight of steps rising above a *sou-bassement*. The two upper storeys and the corners of the building are embellished with *refends*, but otherwise there is only simple surface treatment.

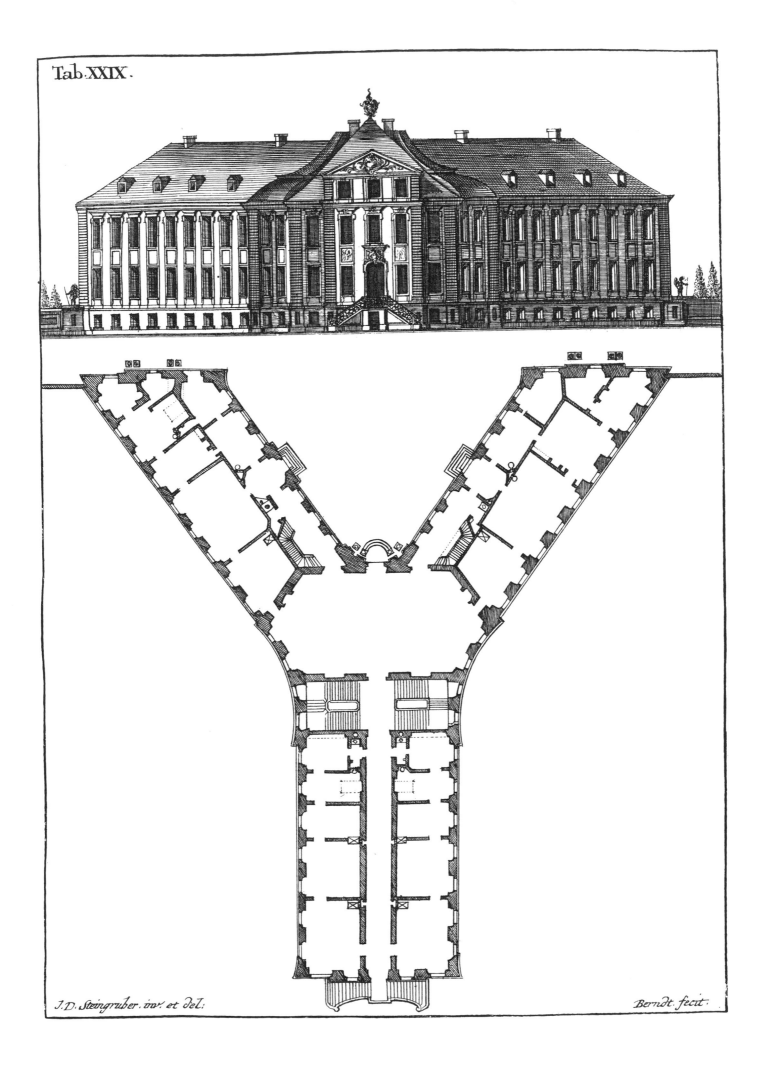

Tab.XXIX.

J.D. Steingruber. inv. et del:

Berndt. fecit.

XXX . Z

UNDOUBTEDLY the character of this last letter is such that again it suffers from the disadvantage of never having served, so far, as basis for a palace plan. But by way of the centrally-placed entry and vaulted entrance hall beyond it, supported on four pillars, the main stairways are so arranged that they are immediately perceptible from both sides, and take up little enough of the available space as they are fitted into otherwise almost unusable angles; and in order to beautify the form of the letter, the sharp, outer corners are somewhat blunted by linking curves. In both corners of the building are round *cabinets*, and within the apices of these same angles are rooms with broken angles, all these adjustments working out in such a fashion that four lordly households could be conveniently lodged in each *étage*.

The façade stands on a raised *socle*, and Ionic pilasters rise through the first two floors. There is an attic storey above, and a roof *à la Mansarde*. So herewith, and even with duplication of letters here and there, the whole alphabet is completed as promised.

Tab·XXX·

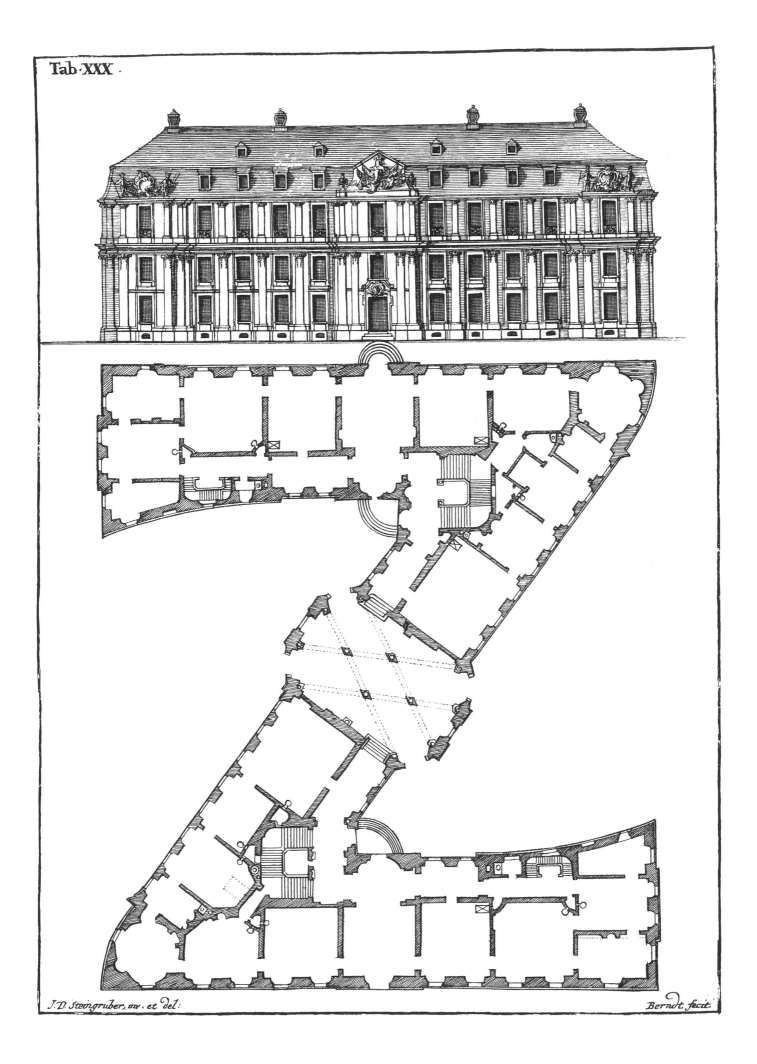

J.D. Steingruber, inv. et del: Berndt fecit

POSTSCRIPT

JOHANN DAVID STEINGRUBER was born on 26 August 1702 at Wassertrüdingen, a village in Brandenburg-Ansbach. The Margrave[1] of this Franconian principality had his Residence and main seat of government in the town of Ansbach, which at that time was also known as Onolzbach.

Steingruber's father, who combined the work of a linen weaver with that of a builder, trained his son as a builder and stone cutter. As was the custom, on completing his apprenticeship he travelled about as a journeyman to gain experience and to perfect himself in his profession, and during this period he made drawings of some of the buildings which interested him.

It is known that he travelled in the Rhineland and that he worked at the building of the palaces of Rastatt and Mannheim.[2] The imposing new town plan of Mannheim must have made a deep impression on the young Steingruber, aspiring as he was to become an architect one day. 'In all the towns he visited during his travels he made himself familiar with the finest buildings and their structure, and with the best masters.'[3]

Above.   A house being built in the country. Stone masons at work in foreground, and on scaffold, laying stones. A gentleman wearing a sword, possibly the architect, supervising the work.
Engraving by Trautner after the design of Johann Amadeus Steingruber (son of J.D.S.)
from Practica . . . *first part, August 1763. Slightly enlarged.*

Postscript

The beginning of the eighteenth century in Germany was an exciting period in architecture. The years of aftermath of the Thirty Years War were past, and it was a time of consolidation and growing prosperity, reflected in the building of palaces, the rebuilding of churches, and the expansion of towns. In Ansbach, during the sixty years of Steingruber's active career there, it was a time of intensive reconstruction and new building. The general aim was to build a new palace, and modernize and expand the town of Ansbach, and so make it a worthy approach and foil to the Margrave's castle.

The first architect on the scene, Gabriel de Gabrieli, with his roots in the Austro-Italian baroque, was called in from Vienna in 1694. He succeeded in transforming the old renaissance castle with its medieval features into a baroque palace with an imposing façade and double-galleried courtyard.

The professional architect de Gabrieli was succeeded by the noblemen Johann Wilhelm von Zocha, director of building from 1715 to 1719, and his brother Karl Friedrich, who acted in the same capacity from 1719 to 1731. Before coming to the capital Johann Wilhelm had been a government administrator[1] at Wassertrüdingen, Steingruber's place of birth, and he may well have encouraged and helped the young Steingruber.

It can be assumed that on his journeying Steingruber learnt, amongst other skills, to work freely in plaster, a decorative medium characteristic of the baroque style, and much used in interiors and on the outsides of buildings. When, at twenty-four, he returned to his home principality he soon found employment in this kind of work and described himself as *Stukkateur*.[2] There is evidence that he brought back with him designs and careful drawings[3] of the palaces of Rastatt and Mannheim, which he showed and later presented to Karl Friedrich von Zocha, the then Director of Building of the Margrave. This proof of Steingruber's skill in architectural drawing, combined with his practical experience in building techniques, must have so convinced von Zocha of the young man's usefulness that in 1726 he accepted him as *Designateur* at the office of works in Ansbach.[4]

The younger von Zocha, a minister of state and councillor to the Margrave, was a 'nobleman skilled and experienced in architectural matters', who originally had studied law at Giessen, Halle, and Leyden. After travel in England, he stayed for some time in France,[5] where he came under the influence of the great architects of Louis XIV, Robert de Cotte (1656–1735) and Jules Hardouin Mansart (1645–1708). Steingruber must have learned a good deal from von Zocha, whose library[6] is reported to have been larger than the Margrave's. It included the most important books on mathematics and, more to the point, a complete collection of works on architectural theory in all languages, both old and new. It must have been stimulating to Steingruber to be taken up by a man with such wide learning and influence,[1] and for his part the courtier must have found the young man sufficiently gifted to warrant his patronage.

In 1734, probably on the recommendation of von Zocha, Steingruber was appointed Inspector of Buildings for the whole of the state of Ansbach.[2] Apart from his official work, which involved a good deal of travel and the supervision of new buildings in the principality, he often received private design commissions from noblemen and gentry.

By 1731 the Italian-born Leopold Retti had succeeded von Zocha in the office of Director of Buildings, and Steingruber continued to help in the execution of various building projects, the most important being the completion of the Residence.

All writers on the architectural history of Ansbach agree that it is difficult to say with certainty to whom the design of many buildings from the seventeen-thirties and forties can be assigned. The architect Leopold Retti completed some of the projects von Zocha had begun and it is a fact that Steingruber, as *Design-ateur*, was also involved in most of these activities. Many gothic churches were rebuilt in a cool and restrained classicist style. The old masonry of towers and foundations was sometimes retained, but the churches themselves were constructed in a plain and dignified style with elegant horseshoe-shaped galleries; great emphasis was always placed on pulpit, organ, and altar to suit the requirements of a Protestant congregation and service. The disciplined baroque style used in these structures had its inspiration in the French Huguenot tradition of that period, in marked contrast to the exuberant baroque of the neighbouring Catholic states.

In 1748 Retti returned to Stuttgart[3] to build the new palace there, and some three years later Steingruber was appointed to be in complete charge of all official building activities in the principality. This job included not only work on the palaces but also the design and building of churches, vicarages, and town halls for many of the smaller towns and villages in the margravate. As the son of a humble village craftsman Steingruber was not officially appointed 'Director of Buildings'. This title meant more than just an impressive distinction, as it carried with it a seat and voice on the Margrave's council of state. To overcome this curious dilemma a building committee[4] was formed under three worthy councillors, but in spite of these restrictions the fact remains that from 1750 onwards Steingruber became head of the office of works and *de facto* chief architect of the state of Ansbach.[5] At the same time he received a small increase in salary.

Throughout the eighteenth century the financial affairs of the small state were precarious. When Margrave Carl Wilhelm Friedrich began his reign in 1729 most of the great building projects, including the Residence,[1] had already been started. The ambitious Carl[2] wanted a splendid palace for himself as well as an equally stylish capital. To achieve this goal the town of Ansbach had to be somewhat modernized and new parts laid out according to a unified plan which had already been suggested by von Zocha. In 1731, to improve the appearance of the town and to stimulate new building Carl decreed special privileges. Depending on the circumstances, building sites were to be presented free, exempt from rates for twenty to forty years, with the cost of building subsidized to the extent of 10–15 per cent. These privileges also applied to the countryside. The only string attached to this ordinance was the stipulation that the prospective house had to be built according to elevations and plans provided free of charge by the Margrave's inspector of buildings, who would also undertake supervision of the work. Moreover when medieval houses had to be rebuilt, after destruction by fire or otherwise, similar directives about the appearance of frontages had to be followed. Here in the capital of a small Franconian state planning practices were already being followed which the Abbé Marc-Antoine Laugier, much admired by Steingruber, did not himself expound until some years later.

'Describing the layout of the streets, Laugier takes up the comparison between garden and town. . . . "The beauty of a park" he points out "does not depend solely on the number, width, and straightness of routes, but on the way in which an architect such as Le Nôtre arranges patterns of all shapes, and combines order with bizarrerie and symmetry with variety, thus making his composition beautiful by means of contrast and even some disorder. The beauty of a town depends in a similar way on an imaginative approach by the planning architect. . . ." He applies the same principle of variety in unity to the houses lining the streets. The design of their façades should not be left to the discretion of private owners, but be laid down by public authority. This authority should fix the height of houses according to the width of the street and see to it that by varying the type of façades from block to block "excessive uniformity, this greatest of all faults," is avoided.'[3]

The effects of these regulations were highly beneficial to the appearance of the town. They did not improve the state finances, but the Margrave's aim was to some extent achieved. According to a chronicler of Ansbach,[4] more than 330 new houses were built in the capital during the five decades from 1732. Including private commissions Steingruber had a hand in most of these developments.

One of the first jobs the newly appointed Inspector of Buildings undertook was to work, with the Building Director Retti, on plans for an extension for the town of Ansbach.[5] Covering this not inconsiderable area with individual houses and carefully-designed terraces was to engage Steingruber's skill for the next fifty years. His private commissions, from roughly the beginning of the seventeen-thirties to the seventeen-fifties, include work not only in Ansbach but also in the surrounding country and even beyond the borders of the principality. They cover designs and suggestions for the alteration and rebuilding of country houses, town halls,[1] and churches. Some of these commissions again came to him through the recommendation of Karl Friedrich von Zocha. Documentary evidence shows that Steingruber was active during this period at Schwäbisch Hall, Windsheim, Coburg, Rentweinsdorf, Rügheim and many other places.

In 1750 he submitted plans and estimates for a new vicarage for the parish of St John in Ansbach. He got into difficulties over this with an aged court official who thought that the new building would darken his view. After various compromises the work was completed four years later. So many drawings had been required for the building that when Steingruber claimed ten Thalers Rhenish for drawing and writing materials, etc. he received in 1756 a hundredweight of corn in lieu of payment.[2]

Coinciding with the new town project was the transformation of an ancient

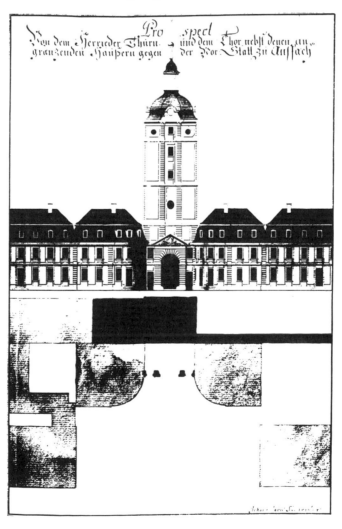

Steingruber's signed drawing for the Herrieder
Gate precinct, about 1750.

town wall site into a fashionable residential area. Modernizing the precinct of the Herrieder Gate, one of the main gates on the south side of the town, was an interesting architectural challenge. In redesigning the tower there Steingruber produced a wonderful focal point as seen from the new town. From a distance it also considerably enriches the silhouette of Ansbach with its older spires and adds a pleasant contemporary counterpart to the solid mass of the castle. The whole tower precinct, completed by Steingruber in 1751, forms a harmonious link between the old and new town. It is a highly civilized translation from the medieval concept of a fortified gate flanked by cylindrical towers into an elegant gate tower with rounded-front dwelling houses on both sides.[1]

This satisfactory use of curved walls is of some importance as it may have given him the assurance some twenty years later to develop it further in his book of architecture based on the straight and curved lines of the Roman alphabet.

When Margrave Christian Friederich Carl Alexander (1736–1806) ascended the throne in 1757 he took on a principality that was not financially sound. Official building activities were very much curtailed, at least at the beginning of the reign. The new Margrave had been educated in Holland, and as a young man had also spent some time in Turin at the court of Savoy. He was an enlightened prince who tried very hard to improve the affairs of his country, which at that time had about 190,000 inhabitants. His occasional travels took him to England[2] (George III was his second cousin) and to France, Switzerland, and Italy.

In 1777 Colonel William Fawcett came to Ansbach to conclude a treaty on behalf of King George for military support in the campaign against the Americans. Over two thousand fully-equipped soldiers and their officers were sent by the Margrave. The money he received from the British government for this service helped to reduce the state debt, which he managed to pay off altogether by the end of his reign.

He was receptive to new ideas. Amongst other things, he tried to improve agriculture by introducing new breeds of cattle, by importing Merino sheep from Spain, and by establishing a stud farm near Triesdorf, his country residence.

Delftware had been manufactured in Ansbach since the beginning of the century, but the setting up of a porcelain factory in the neglected castle of Brucksberg in 1762 can be credited to Margrave Alexander. The sale and export of its products became a not unimportant factor in the economy of the state. The ceramic workshops were kept extremely busy in 1763, when they had to make the 2,800 painted tiles which still cover the walls of the Tiled Hall (Gekachelter Saal) in the Residence at Ansbach.[3] Steingruber supplied the general design for this remarkable interior, as he did for many other rooms in the castle.

Architectura Civilis.

Bestehend in unterschiedlichen Gebäuen, der besten und neuesten Art, nach dem Französchem Gusto, mit gehörigem Grund und Aufrißen samt darzu erforderten Durchschnitten.

Inventirt und gezeichnet von

J. J. Steinburger Archit:

ARCHITECTURE CIVILE
Erster Theil
Bestehent in unterschiedl[ichen]
Zeichnungen, mit gehörigen
Grundt &: Aufrissen &: Darzu
erforderten Profilen
Inventirt u: gezeichnet v. I. D. St.
Kupfer gestochen von
I. G. Ringlin
und verlegt
von I. A. Pfeffel in
Augspurg

Architecture	Civile
premiere	Partie
qui consiste en	divers desseins
avec	leurs
plans et profils;	inventée et dessinée
par	J. D. St.
gravée en	taille douçe
par I. G.	Ringlin,
aux	depens
de I. A.	Pfeffel

Architecture
premiere
qui consiste en
avec
plans et profils
par
graveé en
par J. G.

de J.

Engraved title page of 'Architecture Civile'. Alongside this engraving are shown transcripts
of the wording on it, and a detail from the comparable title page of 'Architectura Civilis'
by J. J. Steinburger, referred to on page 98.

IIIa & b

PRACTICA bürgerlicher Baukunst . . . zum gemein-nützlichen Gebrauch ans Licht gestellet von Johann David Steingrubern . . . Auf dessen Kosten, 1765.
Title, blank, 10 pages of text, engraved title for first part, 20 engravings. Second part: title, blank, 14 pages of text, 15 engravings (the first five and the last as folding double plates). Appendix to second part: title, blank, 14 pages of text, 21 engravings. Third part: title, blank, 10 pages of text, 19 engravings (the seventh and eighth as folding double plates). 4 small engravings at beginning of each section.

All double plates numbered as two. Published in parts. Each part has an address to the reader.

Practische bürgerliche Baukunst . . . ausgearbeitet von Johann David Steingrubern . . . Nürnberg, bey Christian Gotthold Hauffe, 1773.
Frontispiece (engraved title of first part), title, blank, 12 pages of text, 20 engravings. Second part: title, blank, 6 pages of text, 15 engravings (6 as double plates). Appendix to second part: title, blank, 6 pages of text, 21 engravings. Third part: title, blank, 6 pages of text, 19 engravings (2 as double plates). 4 small engravings.

Published as one complete work, therefore the only address to the reader is at the beginning of the book. New edition of IIIa above with identical plates. Size: 24 × 19 cm.

Since the office of the building department failed to provide a further tract (mentioned above), Johann David took over and brought out at his own expense *Practice of Civic Architecture*, etc. (*Practica bürgerlicher Baukunst*, etc.), thus, at personal sacrifice, to some extent redeeming the earlier promise. The book, of quarto size, was issued in three parts, the first of which appeared in August 1763. The complete work with eighty-one copper engravings[1] was not completed before 1765 and contains neither printer's name nor place of publication. Four small engravings used as head pieces are engraved by G. P. Trautner of Nuremberg after designs of J. A. D. Steingruber, the author's son. (See headpiece to Postscript page 86.)

PRACTICA
bürgerlicher
Baukunst

bestehend

in drey Theilen und einem Anhang

denen Liebhabern

der

edlen Baukunst

nach denen

Haupt- und Special-Rissen

und Gesims-Lehren,

zum gemein-nützlichen Gebrauch ans Licht gestellet

von

Johann David Steingrubern,

Hochfürstlich-Brandenburg-Onolzbachischen Bau-Inspectore.

Auf dessen Kosten, 1765.

Practische
bürgerliche
Baukunst

mit den

Haupt- und Specialrissen

und

Gesimslehren,

zum gemeinnützlichen Gebrauch

für

Bauliebhaber, Zimmerleute, Maurer, Tischler rc.

ausgearbeitet,

von

Johann David Steingrubern,

Hochfürstlich-Brandenburg-Onolzbachischen Bau-Inspector.

Mit 76. Kupferplatten.

Nürnberg, bey Christian Gotthold Hauffe, 1773.

The first part of the book deals with designs for an average size house for a country official and for a town house; the second with a nobleman's country house and a church grouped together, and the third with a church. The designs, plans, elevations, and sections are supplemented by the most carefully worked out details for builders, masons, carpenters, joiners, and so on.

The book must have been successful; eight years later a new edition was brought out, in Nuremberg, by Christian Gotthold Hauffe. The title was modified to *Practical Civil Architecture (Praktische bürgerliche Baukunst)* and certain minor adjustments were made to the text. In the preface the author states rather quaintly that civic architecture is one of the noblest aspects of the art of mathematics and that in many countries fine works have been produced which deal with public buildings and splendid palaces, but such publications are too expensive to be generally available. Books published in France on civic buildings are not applicable to the conditions and materials prevalent in Germany, and it is thought desirable that an experienced architect should take the trouble to produce a practical and inexpensive book about this art, easily understood by craftsmen and of interest to their patrons. In the last paragraph of his preface Steingruber mentions that the book has found the approval of two academies. He also refers to his publisher in connection with the project of producing a fourth part at a later date with estimates of costs. C. G. Kayser reported a 1786 Nuremberg edition of the *Practica,* but the writer has not seen this.

IV

Architectonisches ALPHABET bestehend aus dreyssig Rissen . . . von Johann David Steingruber . . . Schwabach, Gedruckt bey Johann Gottlieb Mizler . . . 1773.

Engraved title. Title, blank. Dedication, blank, then dedication continued over 2 pages (1 leaf). 6 pages of address to the reader. 2 double plates and 30 single plates each with a text leaf. A rare prospectus (*Vorbericht*) has 2 pages.

Johann David Steingrubers,

Hochfürstl. Brandenburg = Anspachischen Bau = Inspectorii

Architectonisches Alphabet

Zweyte Abtheilung

bestehend

In fünfzehen Buchstaben Grund= und Aufrissen, nebst deren Erklärung

als

der Schluß des ganzen Alphabets.

Wovon aber

Biß zur künfftigen Ostermesse 1775. die noch weiters angesicherte 18. Blat Kayserl. Königl. Chur= und hoher Fürsten Nahmen, ebenfalls geliefert werden sollen.

From interim title leaf of the second part of 'The Alphabet'. See page 15.

Johann David Steingruber / by appointment, Inspector of Buildings for Brandenburg-Ansbach / ARCHITECTURAL ALPHABET / Second Section / comprising / in fifteen letters, ground plans and elevations accompanied by explanations thereof, / to / complete the whole alphabet, / but to which / by the time of the coming Easter Fair, 1775, the further guaranteed 18 plates based on names of emperors, electors and / royal princes should likewise be added.

Architectonisches
ALPHABET

bestehend

aus dreyßig Rissen

wovon

Jeder Buchstab nach seiner kenntlichen Anlage auf eine ansehnliche
und geräumige Fürstliche Wohnung, dann auf alle Religionen, Schloß=Capellen
und ein Buchstab gänzlich zu einen Closter, übrigens aber der mehreste Theil nach teutscher
Landes=Art mit Einheiz=Stätte auf Oefen und nur theils mit Camins eingerichtet,

wobey auch

Nach den mehrest irregulairen Grund=Anlagen vielerley Arten der Haupt= und Neben=Stie=
gen vorgefallen, dergleichen sonsten in Architectonischen Rissen nicht gefunden werden,

zu welchen auch

Die Façaden mit merklich abwechslender Architectur aufgezogen sind.

Ueber diß

Sind noch zwanzig Plans auf Kayserlich, Königlich, Chur= und
anderer Hoher Fürsten Namen, Risse auf gleiche Art mit aller Geflissenheit und
distincter Architectur dergestalten auf einen Bogen aufgezogen, daß solche eingeschlagen mit denen
vorstehenden in einen Format gebunden werden können.

Hierüber auch so wohl als über erstere

auf jeden Riß zu dessen Eintheilung eine Erklärung

mit einer besondern Vorrede, Titulblat und Dedication
beygefüget worden.

Diese bereits in vielen Jahren zusammen gezeichnete und noch niemalen zum Vorschein gekommene Risse,
werden auf eigene Kosten in drey Transport denen Architectonischen Kennern und curieusen Liebhabern zur geneigten
Einsicht und Aufnahme vorgeleget

von

Johann David Steingruber

vieljährig Hochfürstl. Brandenburg=Anspachischen Bau=Inspector.

Johann Friederich Alexander Steingruben. 1781.

Schwabach,
Gedruckt bey Johann Gottlieb Mizler, Hochfürstl. privil. Buchdrucker.
1773.

NOTES

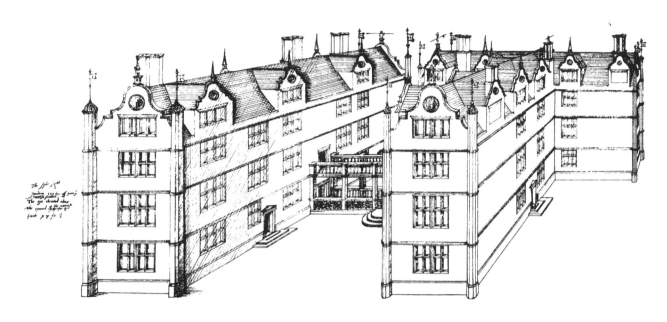

John Thorpe's plan for two linked houses based on his own initials. Detail of elevation.
Sir John Soane Museum, London. See note 15.1 and ground plan page 107.

FRONTISPIECE

Translation of engraved title (page 4): ARCHITEC-
TURAL / ALPHABET / consisting of thirty designs
of plans and elevations / also / twenty imperial royal /
electoral and exalted princes' names / in ground plans
and elevations / also / an explanation of each design /
a preface and dedication / these never seen before /
designed over many years / at [his] own expense /
published / by / [within cartouche] Johann David /
Steingruber / for many years official Inspector of
Buildings to the Prince of Onolzbach.

INTRODUCTION

11.1 *Ansbach*—at that time also spelt Anspach.
11.2 See page 95 for other publications by Steingruber.
11.3 In 1773 a new edition was also published of his
Practica, which he had issued originally at his own

expense (see page 101). The publisher, Christian
Gotthold Hauffe, may have paid Johann David for
the right to publish it and these funds would have
helped him towards bringing out the *Alphabet*. J. G.
Mizler, the printer at Schwabach, was possibly related
to the minister of the same name at Wassertrüdingen,
Steingruber's birthplace.
11.4 60 Kreuzer Rhenish = 1 gulden. The nearest
contemporary equivalent to a gulden was the florin.
11.5 The two double size dedicatory engravings,
each printed from two copper plates and based on the
initials of the author's patrons (C F C A and F C),
may have been originally intended for the third instalment of twenty princely designs. When Steingruber realized the difficulties of achieving this last
section he transferred the two engravings to the
beginning of the *Alphabet*. See page 15.
11.6 Most copies of the *Alphabet* known to the editor
are in their original bindings covered with paste
papers in a variety of single colours and patterns.

11.7 'Orders [for *Architectural Alphabet*] could be sent to the author at Ansbach, to the bookseller Stettin at Ulm, to Herr Hauffe [publisher of the *Practica*], and to Herr Mizler [the printer of the book] at Schwabach.' *Steingruber's prospectus.*

11.8 'The form of building is not sufficiently varied although men differ so widely in their ways of thinking. Will we never desist from slavishly following our predecessors?' Abbé Marc-Antoine Laugier, *Neue Anmerkungen über die Baukunst.* Leipzig, 1768.

Steingruber was much influenced by 'the worthy abbot Laugier . . . so logical and straightforward in his writing on civil architecture'. See also page 89.

14.2 The engraved title page is the only plate of the whole work not engraved by the Nuremberg copper engraver Johann Christoph Berndt (1707–98). Another Nuremberg engraver, Daniel Adam Hauer (1734–89), who is known to have specialized in lettering and maps, was responsible for the engraving of this title. It could well be that engraved illustrative title pieces of this nature could be used by booksellers as display and advertising material. There is a precedent for this in Ben Jonson's *Epigramme III, To my Booke-seller*:

'To lye upon thy stall, till it be sought,
Not offer'd as it made sute to be bought;
Nor have my title-leafe on posts or walls,
Or in cleft-sticks, advanced to make calls.'

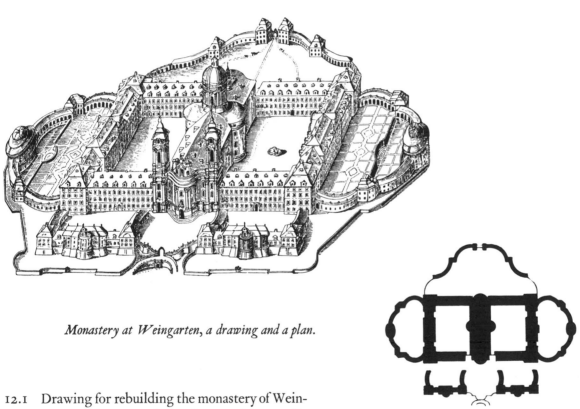

Monastery at Weingarten, a drawing and a plan.

12.1 Drawing for rebuilding the monastery of Weingarten, 1723. The ground plan has an almost calligraphic quality and is shown as an example of the drawing-board architecture of the period.

13.1 Ancient heating arrangements of this kind have been preserved and can still be found in the Residence at Ansbach. See *Ansbach Stadt des fränkischen Rokoko*, Wiedfeld & Mehl, Ansbach, 1966, page 64, and this book page 110.

14.1 In our own time the complete Steingruber alphabet, much reduced, can be seen at a single showing in Massin, *Letter and Image.* Studio Vista, 1970, page 238. (Original edition Paris, Éditions Gallimard, 1970.)

14.3 When peace prevailed in Tudor time the architecture of country and manor houses, even of palaces, underwent a complete change. With the disappearance of the need to combine fortifications with living accommodation, terraces and formal gardens were laid out in carefully designed patterns, and so-called 'knots' replaced moats and defensive walls. In Thomas Hill's *The Gardener's Labyrinth* of 1577, a playful, calligraphic combination of lines provides a typical design for a formal garden.

'The Gardeners Labyrinth . . . Wherein are set forth divers Herbers, Knottes and Mazes cunningly handled for the beautifying of Gardens . . .' by Dydymus Mountaine. London, 1577. Printed and published by Henry Bynneman. Edited by Henry Dethicke. Dedication to Sir William Cecil. (See also *Shakespeare's England*. Clarendon Press, 1917, vol. 1, p. 379.)

14.4   It is just possible that Steingruber had some influence on Anton Glonner's Jesuit College, designed at Strasbourg in 1774 and based on the I H S monogram to form a main and two subsidiary structures.

First reproduced in *Die Christliche Kunst*, Monatschrift für alle Gebiete der christlichen Kunst, Munich, XI, Heft 10, 1915. Since shown in Joseph Ponten, *Architektur die nicht gebaut wurde*, 2 vols., Stuttgart, 1925, II, p. 63, Fig. 132. See also note 15.2 'The various parts were to be employed as follows: the S for school-rooms, the vertical strokes of the H for dining-room and kitchen; the horizontal stroke of the H for the priest's sacristy, the Cross, as centre of the whole, for a church of six domes and many apses.' Ulrich Conrads and Hans G. Sperlich, *Fantastic Architecture*, The Architectural Press, London, 1963, Pl. 119 and note p. 173.

A proper knotte to be cast in the quarter of a Garden, or otherwise, as there is sufficient roomth.

Woodcut of a 'proper knotte' from Thomas Hill, 'The Gardener's Labyrinth', London 1577. Note 14.3.

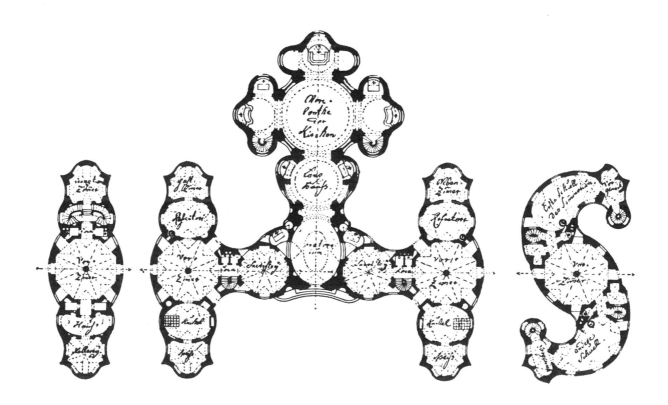

'Dell. et Inv. von Antonij Glonner, in Strasbourg Anno 1774.' Note 14.4.

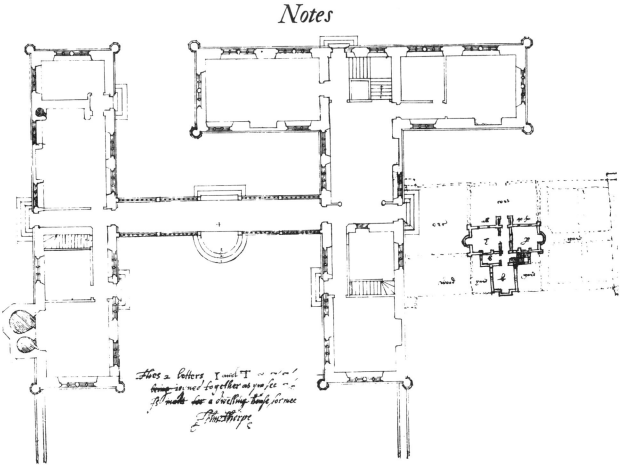

John Thorpe's plan for two linked houses based on his own initials: 'Thes two letters, I and T | being ioyned together as you see | Is ment for a dwelling house for mee | John Thorpe'. *Sir John Soane Museum, London. Note 15.1. For elevation, page 104.*

15.1 John Summerson, *The Book of Architecture of John Thorpe in Sir John Soane's Museum*, The Walpole Society, 1966. Pl. 30b of John Summerson, *Architecture in Britain 1530–1830*, Pelican History of Art, Penguin Books, Harmondsworth, 1953, is of interest in connection with the **H**-shaped plan of Holland House.

15.2 See Ponten, *Architektur die nicht gebaut wurde*, I, pp. 61–63, II, Figs. 126–31. See also note 14.4.

15.3 Pierre Moisy, *Sur une fantaisie architecturale de Thomas Gobert* in *Urbanisme et architecture, Études en l'honneur de Pierre Lavendan*, Paris, 1954.

15.4 Twelve Gulden: about one English guinea.

15.5 The editor is grateful to Herr Adof Lang, the director of the museum and archives of the town of Ansbach, for his courtesy, and for showing him the copy of the *Alphabet* which recounts on its flyleaf the circumstances of Steingruber's gift to the town.

15.6 The name Johann Friederich Alexander Steingruber is written on the title page of the *Alphabet* owned by the editor. See page 103.

15.7 From plate XVI onwards the accompanying text in the original edition of the *Alphabet* is set in a larger size of Fractur type. Moreover the word *Buchstaben* (letter) has been added from O to Y to the large capital letters which head the descriptive matter of the related plates. All this does not necessarily indicate another printer, but a different compositor may have been at work. Possibly the smaller fount was not available at the time, or the larger size type was used to fill the page, as the descriptions become somewhat shorter in the second instalment.

15.8 The engraved and typographic main title envisaged twenty such princely plates. See note 11.5.

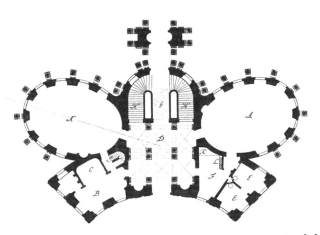

Plate 21 from J. J. Steinburger's 'Architectura Civilis'. A pleasure house in the shape of a crown, ground plan. See overleaf and page 98.

Notes

POSTSCRIPT

86.1 Margrave = *Markgraf*, the sovereign of a German principality.

86.2 The palace at Rastatt was built by Michael Ludwig Rohrer, the one at Mannheim by Clement Froimont and completed by Guillaume d'Hauberat, pupil of Robert de Cotte.

86.3 From the entry in J. A. Vocke, *Geburts- und Totenalmanach Ansbachischer Künstler*, etc., 1792, based on information given by the son Johann Jakob Steingruber, which is one of the rare printed eighteenth-century references to J. D. S.

87.1 *Oberamtmann.*

87.2 Steingruber is given as *Stukkateur* in the entry in the baptismal register of Ansbach referring to his son Johann Jakob.

87.3 Twelve such drawings by J. D. Steingruber are listed in *Catalogus Bibliothecae Zochiana*, vols. I–III, Universitätsbibliothek, Erlangen.

87.4 *Hofbauamt.*

87.5 'Academias Giessae, Haloe Saxonum et Lugduni Batavorum frequentarit, cum florentissimis Europae linguis et loqui et scribere didiceret idem Mathesin dilexit, imprimis Architectonicam militarem pariter ac civilem ita semper coluit, itineribus Gallicis et Anglicis reiteratis auxit et perfecit.' *Catalogus Bibliothecae Zochiana.*

87.6 At the year of von Zocha's death his library contained more than 15,000 volumes.

88.1 Von Zocha was asked by the Prince-Bishop of Würzburg to give a letter of recommendation to Balthasar Neumann to introduce him to his friends in Paris. Karl Lohmeyer, *Briefe Balthasar Neumanns*, 1921.

88.2 *Landbau-Inspektor.*

88.3 Ground plan of the palace in Stuttgart based on a double letter E. →

88.4 *Baudeputation.*

88.5 When in 1769 the margravate of Brandenburg-Bayreuth, through the death of the last prince of the line, came to be united with the one of Ansbach, their respective offices of works kept their independence, each dealing with the buildings in its own territory.

89.1 The castle at Ansbach, like many baroque palaces, is known locally as the *Residenz.*

89.2 Frederick the Great's terse comment on his brother-in-law Carl was that he behaved as though he were Louis XIV.

89.3 From Wolfgang Herrman, *Laugier and Eighteenth Century French Theory*, Zwemmer, London, 1962. This quotation describes and paraphrases certain passages in Laugier's *Essai sur l'architecture*, Paris, 1763. See also note 11.8.

89.4 J. B. Fischer, *Geschichte und ausführliche Beschreibung der Haupt- und Residensstadt Ansbach*, Ansbach, 1786.

89.5 One other instance of Steingruber's collaboration with Retti on a similar scheme can be documented by the plans for a Huguenot colony at Schwabach. They are characteristically signed: Retty inv. Johann David Steingruber delineavit anno 1736.

90.1 The surviving original drawing for the projected town hall of Gunzenhausen is an example of Steingruber's meticulous technique. The town hall was never built but the designs were adapted for a private house. See opposite page.

Ground floor: space for the stands of butchers, bakers, and sundry tradesmen.

First floor: Dance hall, to be used on market days by the weavers [for selling their wares]. Offices of registry, rates, and town chest.

Second floor: Great and small council chambers and administrative offices.

90.2 10 Thalers Rhenish = 15 gulden, about 30s.

91.1 For a modern photograph of Herrieder Gate precinct see *Ansbach Stadt des fränkischen Rokoko*, Wiedfeld & Mehl, Ansbach, 1966, page 20.

91.2 The Margrave's first visit to England was in April 1763.

91.3 For the tiled hall at the Residenz, Ansbach: see Anne Berendsen, etc., *Tiles: A. General History*, Faber, London, 1967, page 258. See also *Ansbach Stadt des fränkischen Rokoko*, Wiedfeld & Mehl, Ansbach, 1966, page 64.

92.1 A riding-school is included in the dedicatory design based on the Margrave Alexander's initials.

93.1 Biarelle was responsible for much of the decorative work in the rococo style in the Residence at Ansbach. Many of these interiors were executed under the supervision of Steingruber.

93.2 See *Jahrbuch des Historischen Vereins für Mittelfranken* vol. 82, Ansbach, 1964/5, pp. 181–9.

93.3 A copy of this document is in the Staats-Archiv Nürnberg, MBA 701.

94.1 Anna Barbara née Schiller, widow of organ builder Prediger. Both Steingruber's wives were called Anna Barbara, as was his mother.

94.2 Johann Jakob Steingruber worked in Rome (at St Peter's) from 1752 to 1763, and married a Roman.

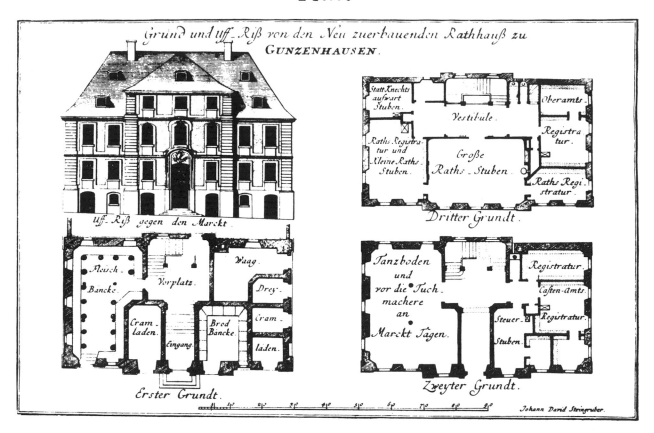

*Steingruber's design (one of ten) for a town hall at
Gunzenhausen. Note 90.1.*

On his return to Ansbach he worked as *Designateur*
and assistant to his father.

94.3 Johann Amadeus Steingruber designed the
frontispiece and probably the illustrations, engraved
by A. Hoffer, to *Der vollkommene Pferdekenner*, Uffen-
heim, 1764; see also headpiece to Postscript, page 86.

94.4 Lady Elizabeth Craven (1750–1828), a daugh-
ter of the fourth Earl of Berkeley, first married William
Craven in 1767, and Margrave Alexander in 1791, a
month after Lord Craven's death. She had many
talents, and wrote a number of light plays and her
autobiography, *Memoirs of the Margravine of Anspach*.

94.5 *Briefe eines Weltbürgers*, etc., Palm, Erlangen,
S.D. (*c.* 1793).

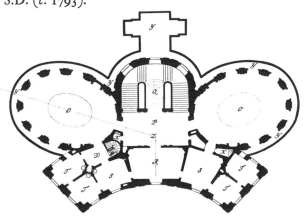

BOOKS BY J. D. S.

95.1 Georg Andreas Böckler was the only other
amongst the court architects of Ansbach to produce
books on architecture (from 1648 to 1688). He was
architect to the Margrave from 1679 to 1698. His
first book was *Compendium Architecturae Civilis*, Strasbourg, 1648.

98.1 J. A. Pfeffel (1674–1748) was also the publisher
of the works of Salomon Kleiner.

98.2 According to Peter Jessen in *Der Ornamentstich*,
Berlin, 1920, the elder de Cuvilliés studied for some
years at the academy of de Cotte in Paris. As von
Zocha also came under the influence of this master
the inclusion of the Cuvilliés projects in Steingruber's *Practica* is of some interest.

100.1 *Practice of Civic Architecture*: the introductions
to the various parts with their supplements carry
the following dates: Part I, 26 Aug. 1763; Part II,
3 April 1764; 28 April 1764; 31 Aug. 1764, 8 Sept.
1764; Part III, 30 Dec. 1764.

*Plate 22 from J. J. Steinburger's 'Architectura Civilis'.
First floor of a building in the shape of a crown. See
preceding leaf and page 98.*

Iron canon stove fed from corridor outside the room.
Engraving from Practica . . . *appendix to second part,*
August 1764, page 13. See note 13.1

ACKNOWLEDGEMENTS

People and Institutions

The editor and publishers have received help and encouragement from many sources during the production of this book. They would particularly like to thank Paul Breman, K. E. Butler, Geoffrey Ireland, Adolf Lang, M. Massin, Michael Pächt, Dr Hugo Schnell, Gustav Stresow, Patricia Verity, and Ben Weinreb; The German Institute London, Stadtarchiv Ansbach, Schlossbibliothek Ansbach, Bayerische Staatsbibliothek Munich, Bibliothek der Technischen Hochschule Munich, and Universitätsbibliothek Göttingen.

Books and Documents

Friedrich H. Hofmann, *Die Kunst am Hofe der Markgrafen von Brandenburg,* Fränkische Linie. Strasbourg, 1901.

Eduard Knorr, *Johann David Steingruber, ein markgräflicher Baumeister des 18. Jahrhunderts.* Thesis 1922. Technische Hochschule, Munich.

Friederich Vogtherr, *Geschichte der Stadt Ansbach.* Ansbach, 1927.

Eugen Maria Hausladen, *Der markgräfliche Baumeister Joh. David Steingruber und der evangelische Kirchenbau.* Ansbach, 1930.

Adolf Bayer, *Die Ansbacher Hofbaumeister* beim Aufbau einer Fränkischen Residenz. Würzburg, 1951.

Günter Schuhmann, Markgraf Alexander von Ansbach-Bayreuth, 1736–1806. Exhibition Catalogue, Ansbach, 1956.

Günter P. Fehring, *Stadt und Landkreis Ansbach.* Munich, 1958.

Heinz Braun, Sommerresidence Triesdorf II. Baugeschichte der Anlagen. Kallmünz, 1958.

Erich Bachmann (editor), *Residenz Ansbach,* Official Guide. Munich, 1962.

III